THE BEST OF
NEW
CERAMIC
ART

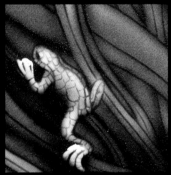

Featuring Winners of the

Monarch National Ceramic Competition

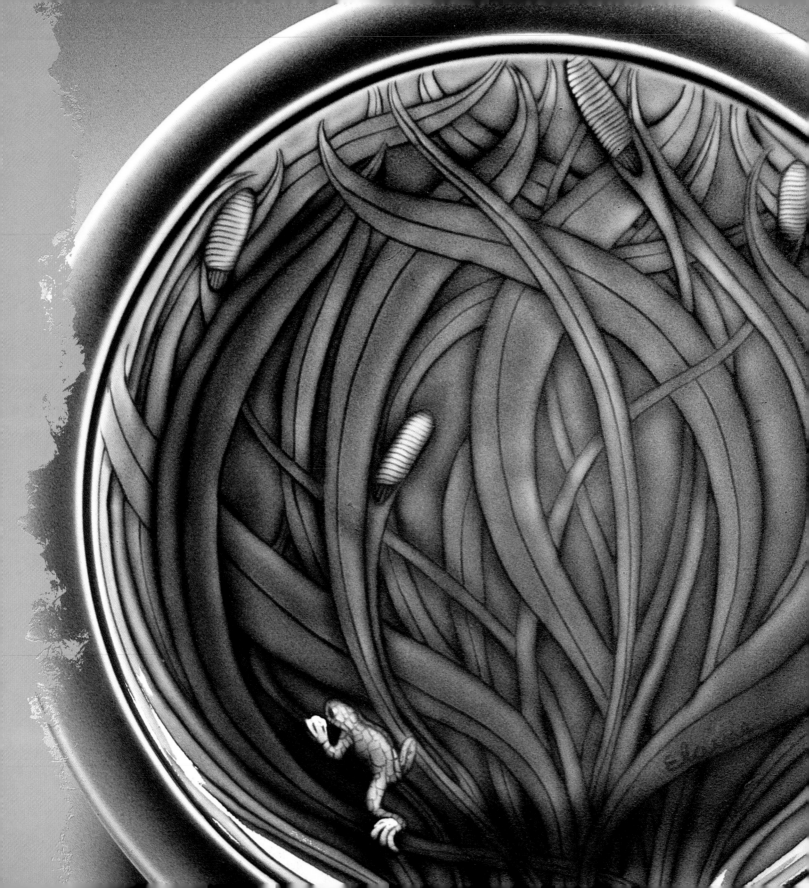

THE BEST OF
NEW CERAMIC ART

Featuring Winners of the

Monarch National Ceramic Competition

Hand Books, Inc.

THE BEST OF NEW CERAMIC ART

Published by Hand Books, Inc., a joint venture of
THE GUILD and Design Books International
931 E. Main Street, #106
Madison, WI 53703
Telephone: (608) 256-1990, (800) 969-1556
FAX: (608) 256-1938

ISBN: 1-880140-28-4

U.S. Distribution: North Light Books,
an imprint of F&W Publications
1507 Dana Avenue, Cincinnati, OH 45207
Telephone: (513) 531-2222, (800) 289-0963

Overseas Distribution: Hearst Books International
1350 Avenue of the Americas, New York, NY 10019

Writer and Editor: Toni Fountain Sikes
Editorial Assistance: Katie Kazan, Jennifer Thelen
Design and Production: Stephen Bridges
Distribution Coordination: Design Books International

Kennedy-Douglass Center for the Arts:
Barbara K. Broach, Director; Mary Nicely, Curator;
Karle Tolbert, Administrative Assistant

Front Cover: Jeri Hollister, *Iron Tribute*
Back Cover (clockwise from top): Lana Wilson, *Artifact Teapot*;
Jean Cappadonna-Nichols, *Napoleon with Red Face and Green Fish*;
Peter Pinnell, *Straw Teapot*; Amy M. Nelson, *Woman as Icon* (detail);
Katharine Gotham, *Bullet Pot*

Page 2: Elaine Coleman, *Incised Porcelain Frog Plate*
Page 5: Beverlee Lehr, *Blue Horizon: Sanibel Island* (detail)
Page 8: Roxie Ann Worthy, *Minoan Bull*
Page 10: Elizabeth MacDonald, *Gold Wheel with Tiles*
Page 14: Jeri Hollister, *Iron Tribute*
Page 38: Leslie Lee, *More Mending*
Page 60: David Stabley, *Wall Tile Composition*
Page 80: Robin Johnson, *Homage to Scully*
Page 110: Jason Hess, *Twelve Whiskey Cups*

Printed and bound in Singapore

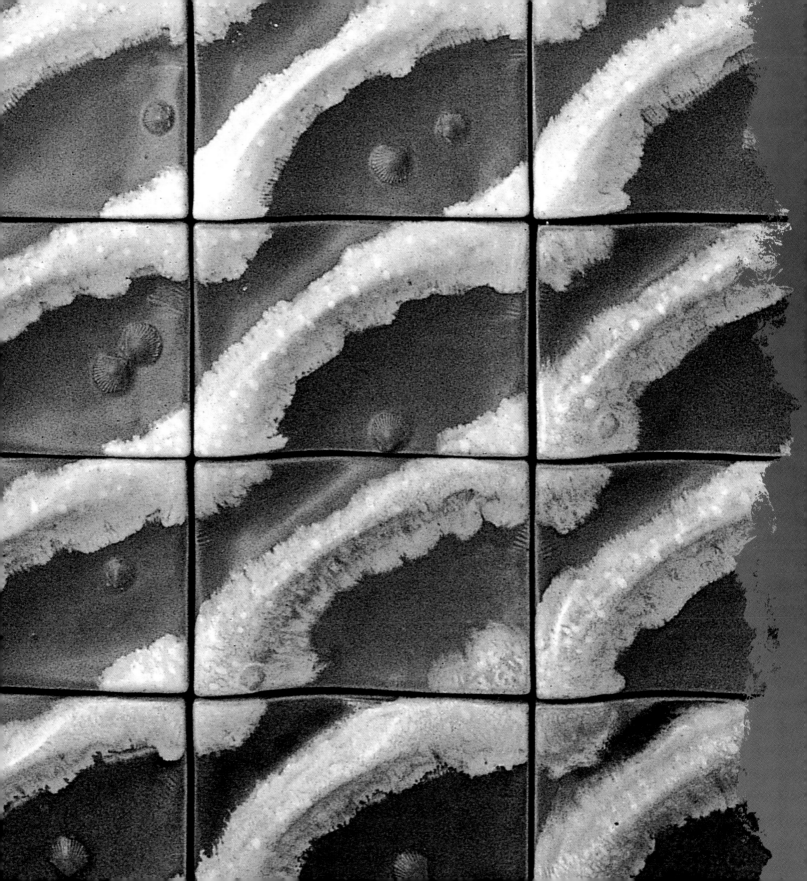

ARTISTS BY SECTION

TABLE OF CONTENTS

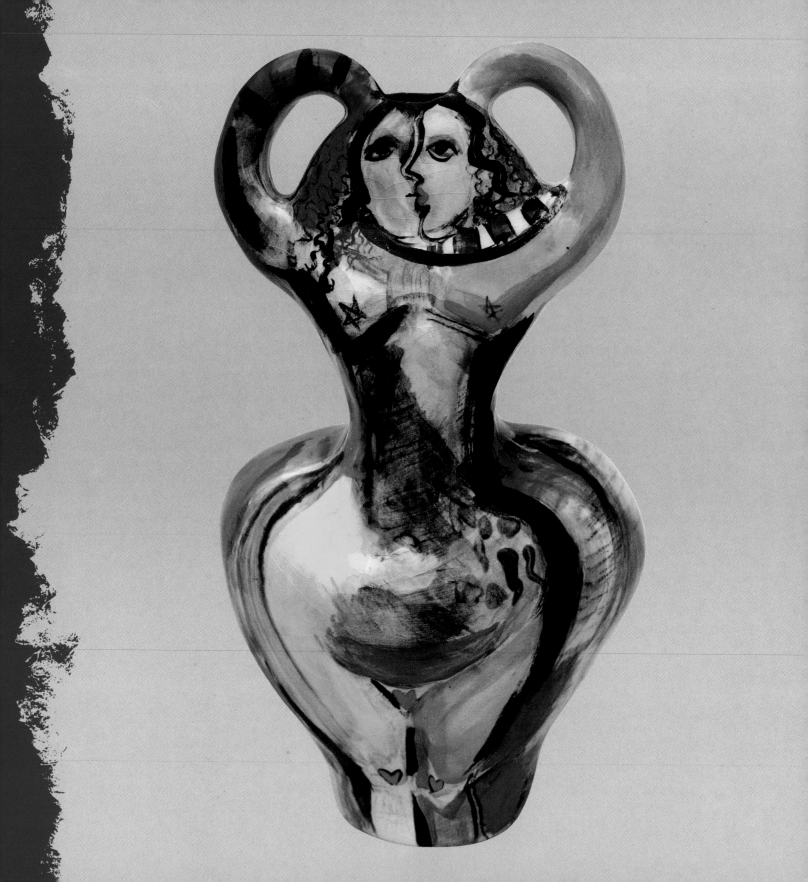

INTRODUCTION

For ten years Monarch Tile has sponsored the Monarch National Ceramic Competition. During this time the competition has grown in stature and reputation — to the point where today it is one of the premiere competitions for showcasing outstanding new ceramic art in North America.

As the invited juror for the 1996 competition, I spent many, many hours viewing slides of almost 1,000 entries from all over North America. My role was to select a body of the best work, all made within the previous year, that would reflect the vitality of the ceramics field.

In years of jurying shows and exhibitions, I have never faced such a daunting task. When I finally made the journey to view the selected pieces in exhibition, I was struck, once again, by the strength and depth of this group of winning pieces. The entire exhibit made an important statement about new American ceramics. And this was a statement that should be presented beyond the physical exhibition itself.

Thus this book. Think of it as an exhibition on paper, where one can move between the rooms at will — and then revisit at a later date. What a broad range of talent! There are the beautifully serene, functional pieces. There is quite a bit of work with exciting new aesthetics, including work for the wall as well as the pedestal. And some very strong, challenging sculptural work.

People sometimes look wistfully at pieces of ancient ceramics in museums as if this art form were lost and buried. Yes, it takes an incredible amount of creativity to make ceramic art that adds to this remarkable history. The Monarch National Ceramic Competition is robust evidence that masterworks continue to be produced.

I congratulate the talented artists, and applaud Monarch Tile for sponsoring this competition. Their efforts bring recognition to a deserving group of ceramic artists. — TONI FOUNTAIN SIKES

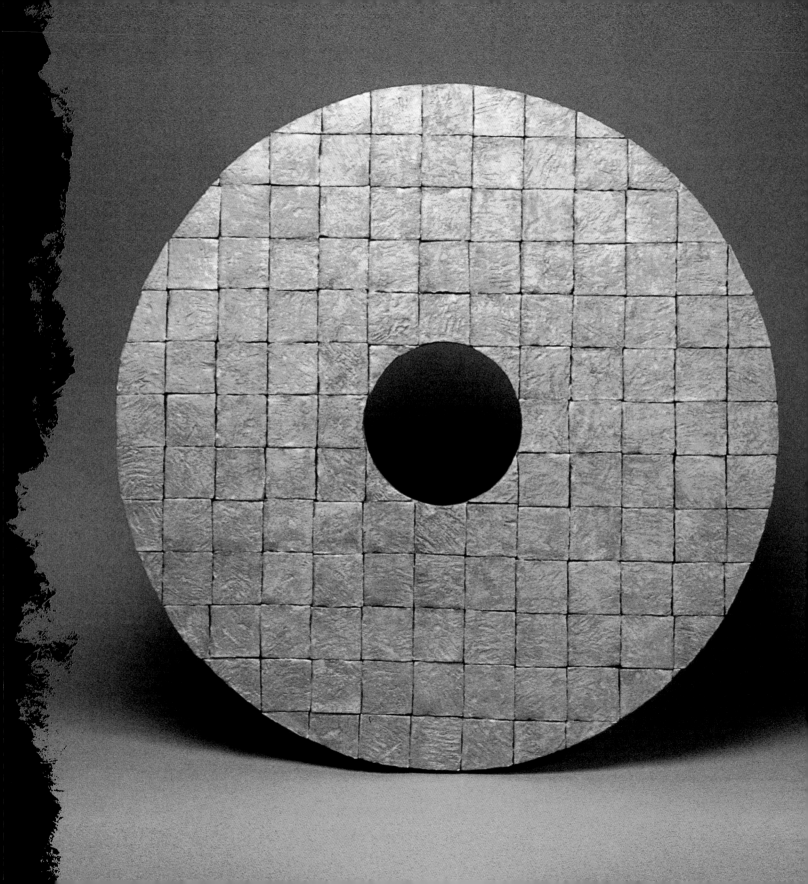

HISTORY

A brief history of the Monarch National Ceramic Competition

It is somehow fitting that Monarch Tile, Inc., the world's fourth largest manufacturer of ceramic wall tile, is the founding and continuing sponsor of one of the premier competitions of ceramic art in North America. After all, both Monarch Tile and the artists they support create products from the same stuff. Through this competition, Monarch Tile showcases and celebrates the achievements of artists and what they create using the most basic ingredients of mud and water.

The first Monarch National Ceramic Competition was held in San Angelo, Texas in 1986, where the company was then headquartered. Initiated by Barba Squire Keene, Monarch's far-sighted Marketing Services Manager, the competition's purpose — to encourage an understanding and respect for the use of clay for both building and artistic purposes — is still in place today. Then, as now, Monarch Tile fully underwrites the venture and provides the more than $5,000 in prize money that is awarded.

The competition was coordinated by the San Angelo Museum of Fine Arts — where the exhibition of selected pieces was also shown. Museum director Howard J. Taylor and his staff deserve credit for nurturing and growing the competition into a major presence, one that included artists' work from Canada and Mexico as well as the United States.

In a field where there are few opportunities for artists to showcase new work, the Monarch National Ceramic Competition quickly filled a real need — offering a forum to ceramists at all career levels to have their work seen in a significant, widely publicized context. Each annual exhibition was a major survey of the field, causing American Ceramics magazine to write in 1989, ". . . if you want to see what's going on in American ceramics, this is it."

In 1989 Monarch Tile moved their corporate headquarters to Florence, Alabama, and in 1995 the competition moved there also. Thomas White, Monarch's President and Chief Executive Officer, approached the Kennedy-Douglass Center for the Arts in Florence about assuming responsibility for coordination of what had become a major annual event.

In the last few years, the competition, has grown qualitatively and quantitatively. It has also furthered the careers and enhanced the reputations of innovative artists who make everything from large sculptural pieces to delicate tea cups.

Housed in a beautiful, old Southern mansion in downtown Florence, the Kennedy-Douglass Center for the Arts is important arts center and exhibition space in North Alabama. Under the leadership of Barbara K. Broach, Director of the Florence Department of Arts and Museums, the capable staff of the Center organizes and publicizes the competition, coordinates the jurying process, and lovingly displays the selected pieces in exhibition.

In the process, they provide a megaphone to tell the world about the vitality of new American ceramics. It is to Monarch Tile's credit and to everyone's benefit that this remarkable work is now seen by an appreciative international audience.

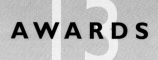

AWARDS

FIRST PLACE

Jeri Hollister   35

SECOND PLACE

Fleur E. Reynolds   56

THIRD PLACE

Lana Wilson   113

TILE AWARD

Elizabeth MacDonald   69

MERIT AWARDS

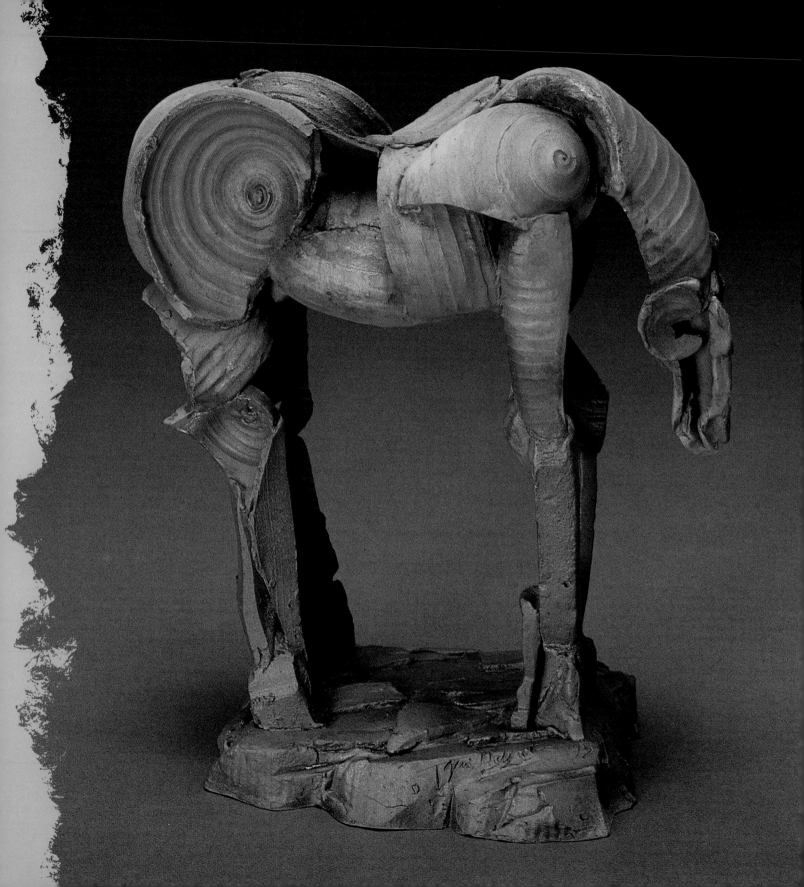

SCULPTURE IN CERAMICS 15

In a sense, all art addresses the issue of how the artist and the audience see. This is even more true when the art is made of that most humble of elements — earth — because the process of creation also becomes part of the viewer's experience.

Clay has no form of its own, but its polymorphous nature offers unlimited prospects for the contemporary artist to make a personal statement. Attracted by clay's malleability and mutability, a growing number of artists are exploiting its sculptural potential.

The journey from idea to image calls upon years of developing the necessary skills. But it is the resolution of form and the communicative power of the image itself that is paramount. Each of these works relies on strong technique, but each goes beyond technique to serve as a vehicle for expression. The artists have succeeded in translating form into sculptural works that are outstanding because of their honesty and courage.

The sculptures created by these award-winning artists is as diverse as the medium allows — ranging from the abstract to the representational, from the quiet and minimal to the shockingly dramatic. A few of these works are disarmingly simple, and yet manage to illuminate an inner core of meaning. Others make reference to further contexts and provide entry to different worlds. The strongest pieces display a highly complex layering of reality and illusion.

The core connection among this disparate group of artists is that each has successfully developed a personal, visual language by manipulating clay, not unlike the way writers manipulate words. Their works not only speak to us, they exclaim, question and talk back!

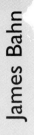

James Bahn

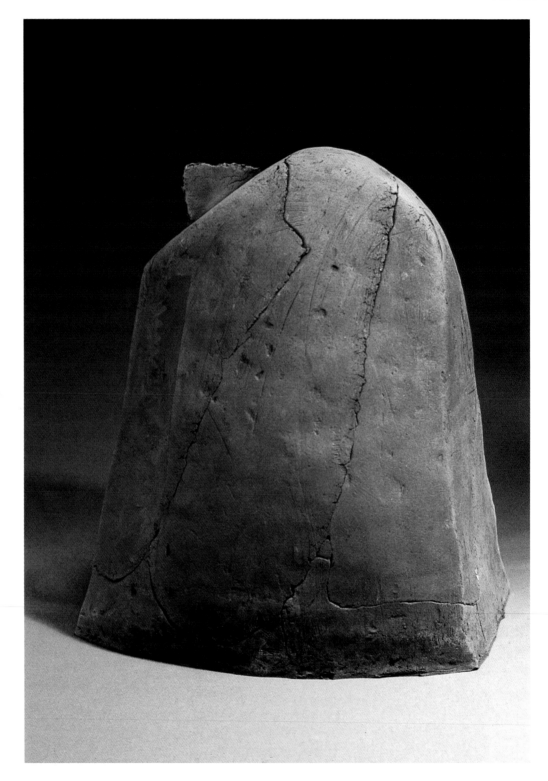

ARTIST: James Bahn
TITLE: Memorial Figure 9
DIMENSIONS: 16.5" x 15" x 12"
MATERIALS/TECHNIQUES: Earthenware,
reduction fired

This piece is part of a series of figures
exploring the loss of friends and family.
It reflects a tombstone-like memorial to a
friend who is dead inside. A rough symbol
on the surface represents damage to her
soul.

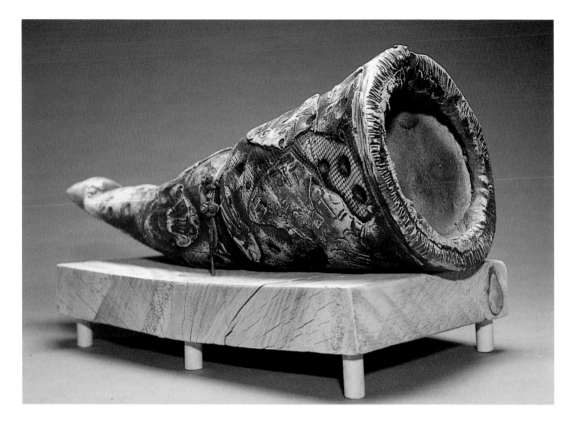

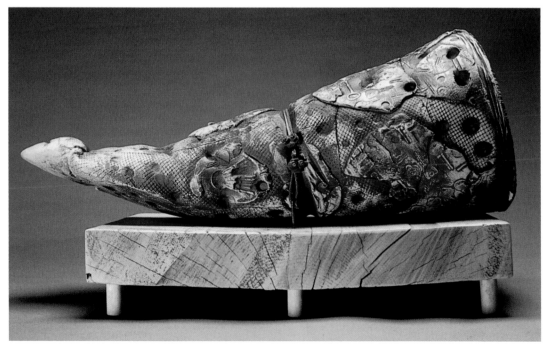

Brian Christensen

ARTIST: Brian Christensen
TITLE: Where Lost Keys Go
DIMENSIONS: 15" x 32" x 15"
MATERIALS/TECHNIQUES: Fired
stoneware, fastened to wood bench
by steel cable

Hanna Jubran

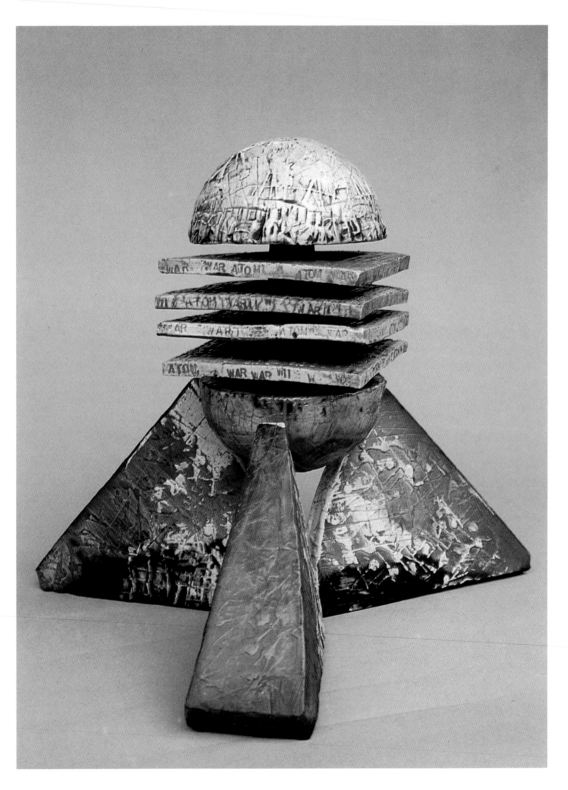

ARTIST: Hanna Jubran
TITLE: Ground Zero
DIMENSIONS: 18" x 23" x 23"
MATERIALS/TECHNIQUES: Ceramic, raku,
low-fire glaze, hard slab

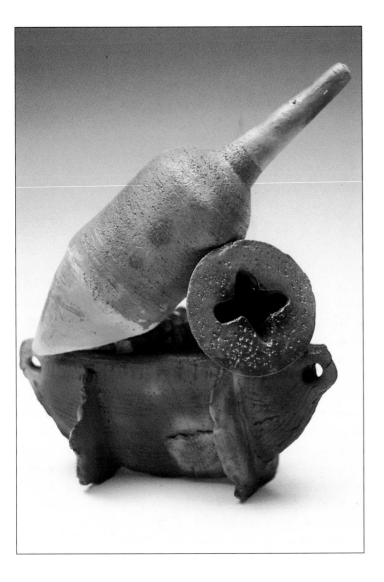

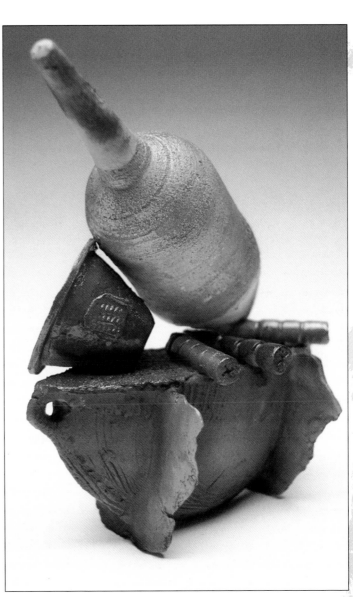

ARTIST: Gerald G. Smith III
TITLE: Lost Ark
DIMENSIONS: 16" x 13" x 5"
MATERIALS/TECHNIQUES: Low-fire clay,
slips, underglaze, low-fire soda

Keith Bryant

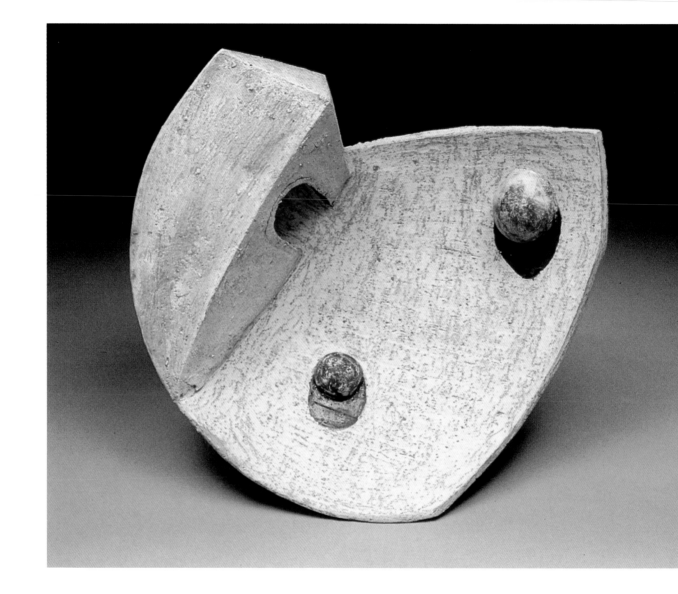

ARTIST: Keith Bryant
TITLE: Two Spheres
DIMENSIONS: 20" x 20" x 6"
MATERIALS: Stoneware
TECHNIQUES: Slump molded slab,
multi-fired

Bryant explores ideas based on two-dimensional compositions involving architecture
and landscape. Surface is an important
component in his work, with a palette limited
to muted earth tones.

Sandra Luehrsen

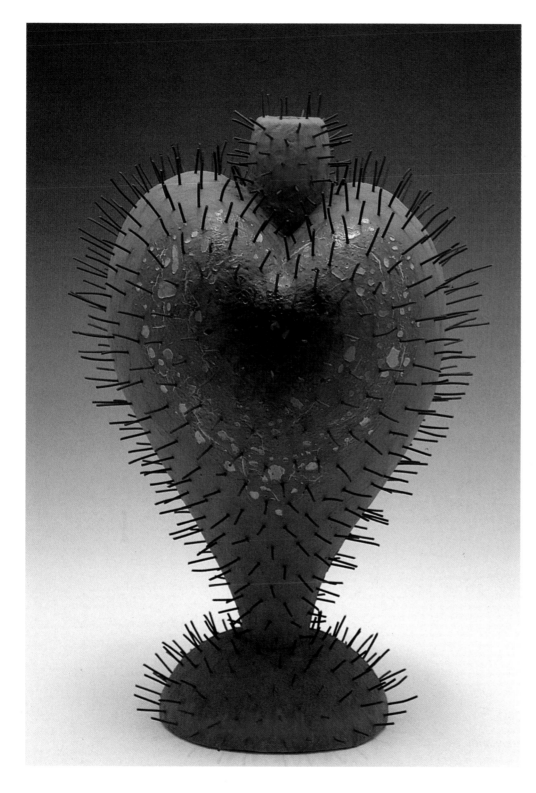

ARTIST: Sandra Luehrsen
TITLE: Jealous Heart
DIMENSIONS: 16" x 10" x 5"
MATERIALS: Ceramic terra cotta,
slips, glazes
TECHNIQUES: Slab built, coil built, carved

Luehrsen explores symbolic and anatomical
heart forms to convey the complex emotions of relationships.

Mandy Greer

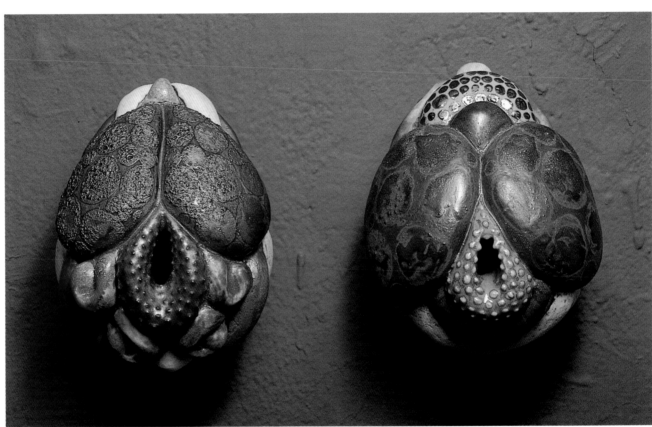

Photo: Andy Nassise

ARTIST: Mandy Greer

TITLE: Lovers

DIMENSIONS: 3.5" x 2.5" x 2"

MATERIALS: Porcelain

TECHNIQUES: Gas-fired reduction, hand built, carved

Greer is fascinated by the link between women and ritual to body decoration, from the Egyptian scarab jewels to Polynesian tatoos. She works on a small scale, with seashell, snake and bug forms. Their patterns remind her of the human desire to decorate the body.

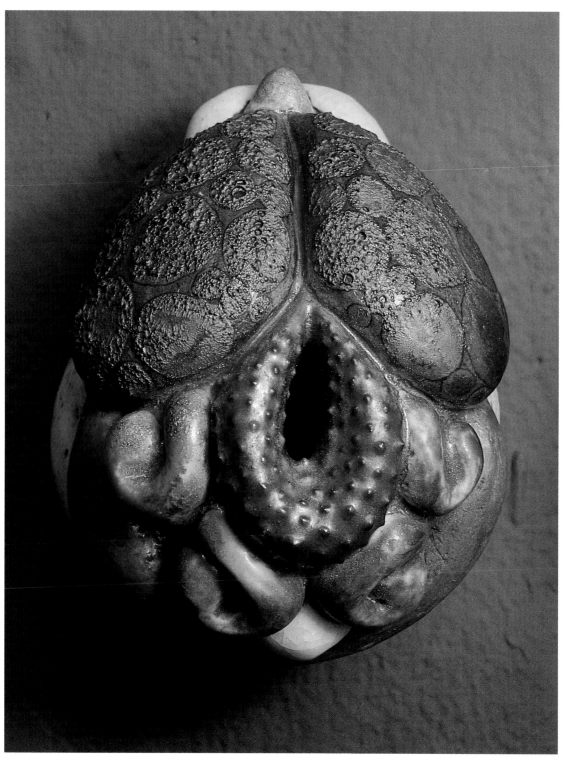

Lisa Maher

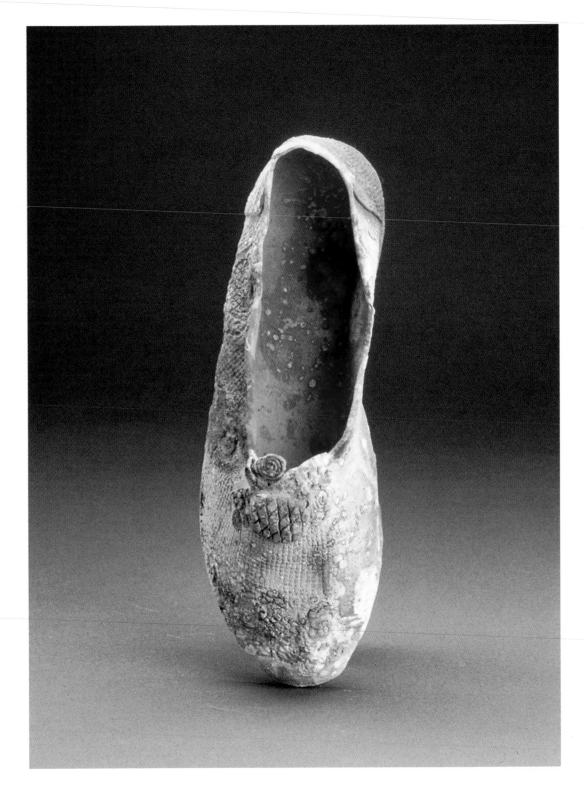

ARTIST: Lisa Maher

TITLE: Shoe

DIMENSIONS: 9" x 2.5" x 2.5"

MATERIALS: Stoneware

TECHNIQUE: Saggar-fired

Maher takes everyday objects that have strong personal meanings, and to which people can easily relate, and transforms them into sculptural work.

Photo: Raymonde Bergeron

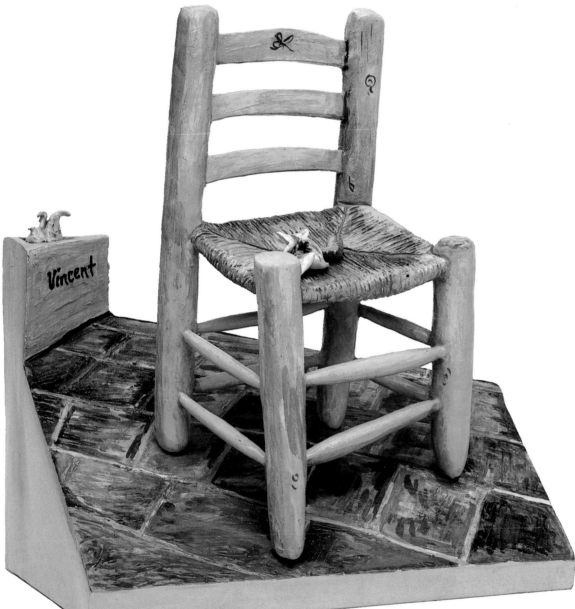

ARTIST: Claire Salzberg
TITLE: Van Gogh's Chair
DIMENSIONS: 12" x 12" x 8"
MATERIALS/TECHNIQUES: Ceramic,
low fire, low-fire glaze

Salzberg loves making chairs and is particu-
larly fascinated with van Gogh. In this
piece, she shows his skewed vision in three
dimensions.

Susannah Israel

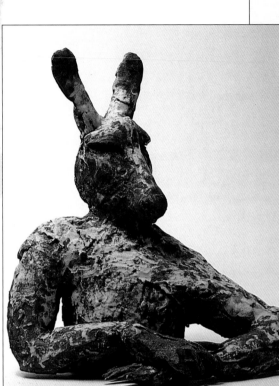

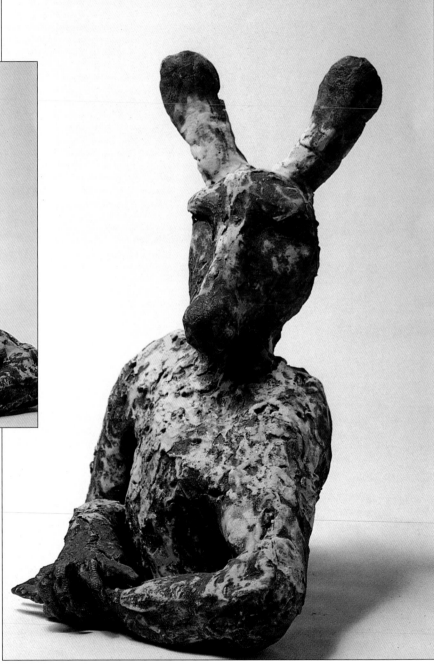

ARTIST: Susannah Israel

TITLE: Dreamtime #3

DIMENSIONS: 20" x 30" x 22"

MATERIALS/TECHNIQUES: Clay, hand
built, slips, oxide

Israel's Dreamtime series was inspired by
a snapshot of a sleepy kangaroo, lying on its
side, regarding the photographer with a
drowsy, curious gaze. The unusual posture
and expression made the beast look like an
enchanted human.

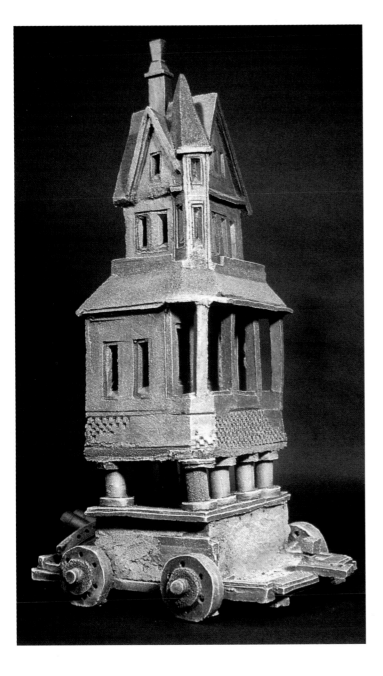

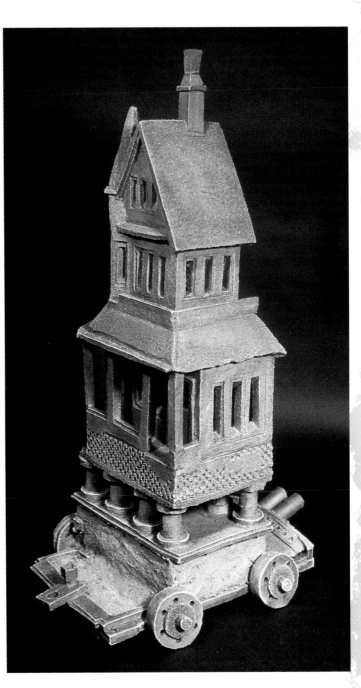

Charles Johnson

ARTIST: Charles Johnson
TITLE: Mobile Home
DIMENSIONS: 35" x 15" x 12"
MATERIALS: Mid-range sculpture clay, unglazed
TECHNIQUES: Hand built

This piece is part of an ongoing series that mixes toy-like qualities with architecture, animals and other objects. The base seemingly supports the whole structure, which creates a physical tension within the piece.

James J. Brashear

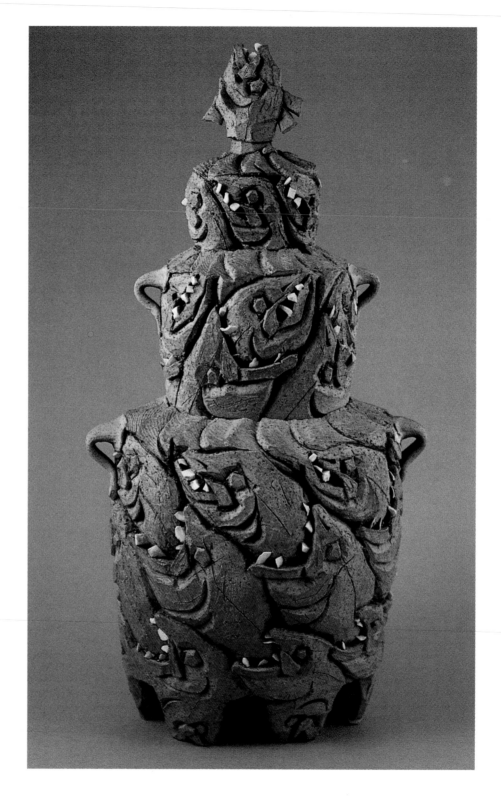

ARTIST: James J. Brashear
TITLE: Reliquary I, Fish Eat Fish World
DIMENSIONS: 22" x 14" x 7"
MATERIALS/TECHNIQUES: Clay, sand,
bronze, thrown, altered, carved

C.A. McWeeny

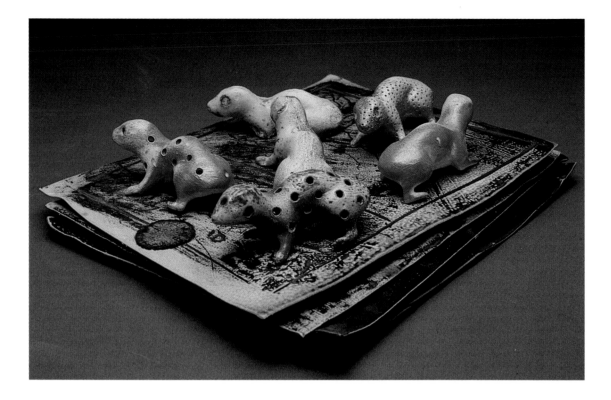

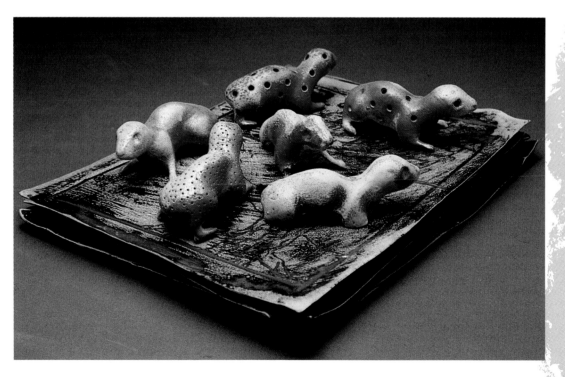

ARTIST: C.A. McWeeny
TITLE: Untitled Diary
DIMENSIONS: 4" x 8.5" x 11"
MATERIALS/TECHNIQUES: Porcelain,
soda fired

Beth Changstrom

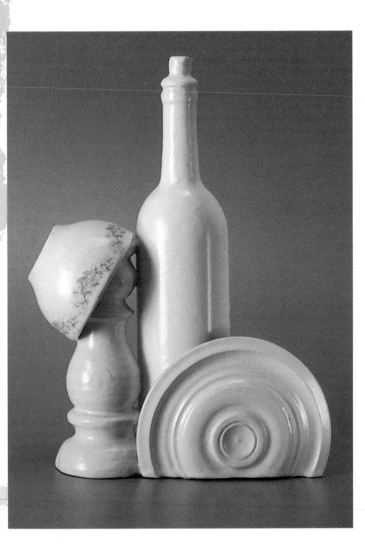

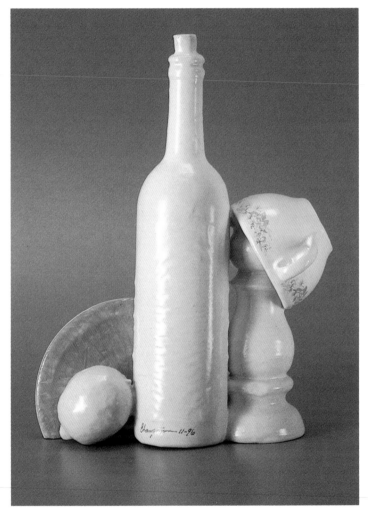

ARTIST: Beth Changstrom
TITLE: Buster
DIMENSIONS: 12.5" x 9" x 4.5"
MATERIALS/TECHNIQUES: Low-
temperature ceramic, thrown, cast, glazes,
overglazes

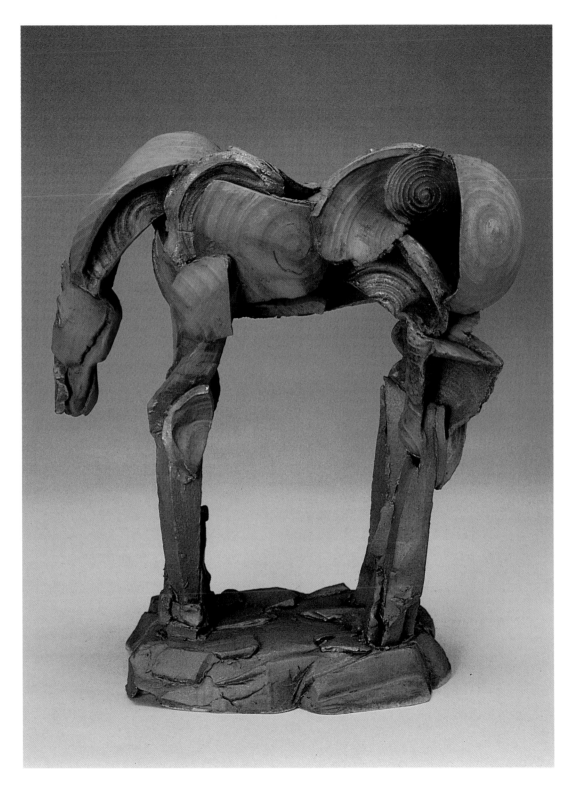

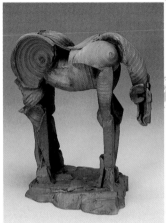

ARTIST: Jeri Hollister
TITLE: Iron Tribute, 95-2
DIMENSIONS: 15" x 13" x 7"
MATERIALS: Earthenware
TECHNIQUES: Wheel-thrown forms altered and combined with hand built forms

For Hollister, the horse is a personal symbol, providing her with strength and direction. She seeks to embody the evidence of the ceramic process as well as the physical and historical attributes of the animal. Her sources include Japanese Haniwa and Chinese Han and Tang Dynasty sculpture, as well as the contemporary horse imagery of Deborah Butterfield, Susan Rothenberg and Pablo Picasso.

Keith S. Mitchell

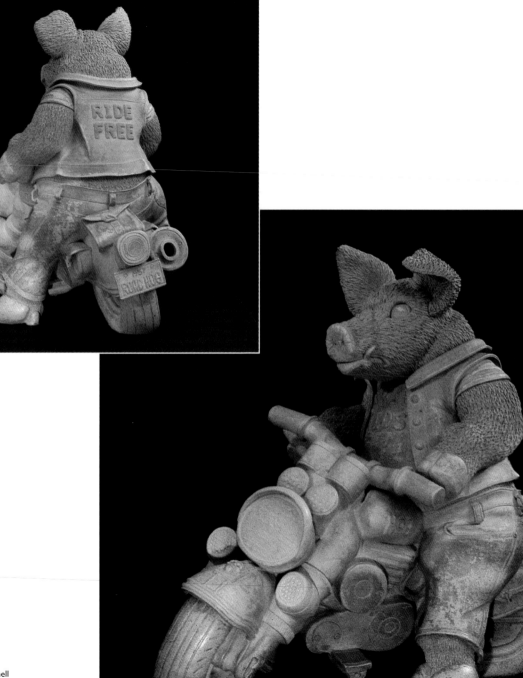

ARTIST: Keith S. Mitchell
TITLE: The Road Hog
DIMENSIONS: 34" x 28" x 18"
MATERIALS/TECHNIQUES: Stoneware,
hand built

Diane L. Sullivan

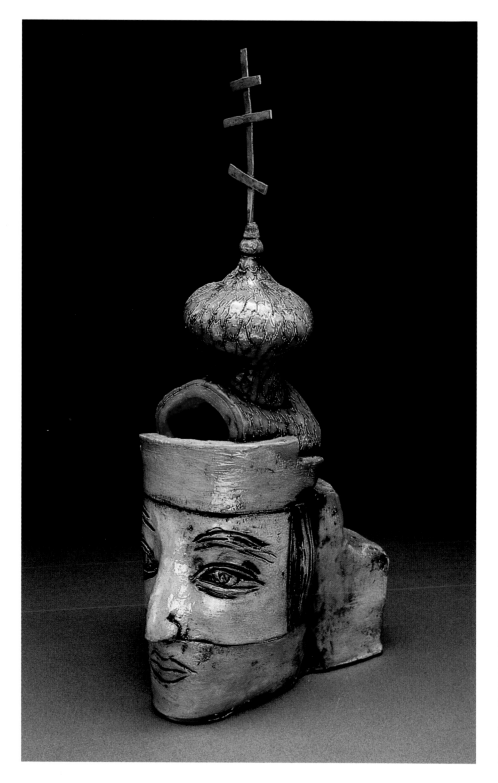

ARTIST: Diane L. Sullivan
TITLE: Her Home is Russia
DIMENSIONS: 13" x 4" x 6"
MATERIALS/TECHNIQUES: Salt-glazed
stoneware, hand built

Sullivan uses the head as her main form.
Ancient architecture and shrines from
foreign cultures inspire her as well.

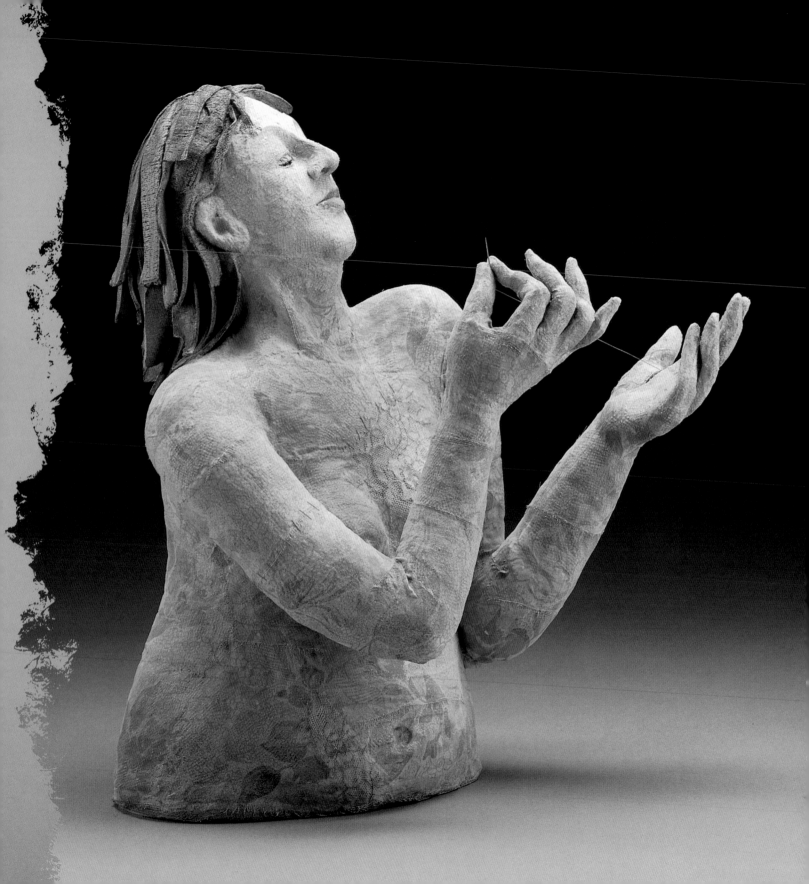

THE CLAY FIGURE

In Cynthia Ozick's story, "Puttermesser and Xanthippe," the protagonist forms a woman out of raw earth, animating her by blowing air gently into her nostril. Similarly, the artist's generative powers give life to the clay figure.

Taking advantage of the versatility and expressive potential of clay, these artists create flesh using the earthy, warm tones of the medium. Pieces are built, modeled and carved, exploiting the clay's tendency to form visceral folds and fissures.

The figural language of these ceramic artists provide us with an exciting array of sculptures. Whether a representational figure, or figurative expressionism, each piece succeeds in making an intensely human statement.

The greater number of sculptures in this group speak to issues of gender. This is not so surprising, as the majority of practicing ceramic artists are women who, like other professionals, must balance the roles of homemaker and wage earner. In these pieces, the struggle is revealed with autobiographical elements and a feminist sensibility. Several of the sculptures address the traditional sphere of women's work, while others make an oblique reference to the feminine role. Whether a piece portrays a woman overwhelmed by the laundry or a figure lounging at rest, the distinct expressiveness captured in the clay is powerful.

The human form has the ability to evoke the most emotional of responses. Each of these clay figures can be viewed as a universal metaphor for the human condition. At the same time, as the artist's intent and content converge, each figure speaks to the individual viewer in a very private way.

Barb E. Doll

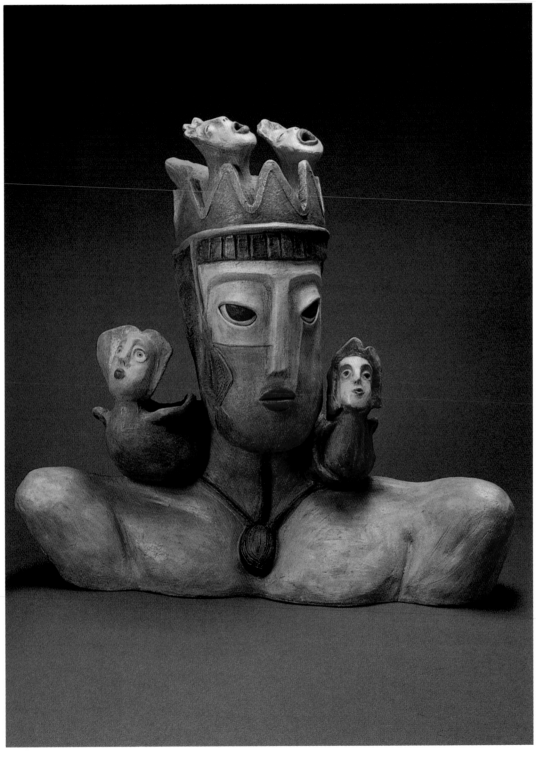

ARTIST: Barb E. Doll

TITLE: Growth and Potential

DIMENSIONS: 30" x 28" x 16"

MATERIALS/TECHNIQUES: Clay, oils

Photo: Bart Kasten

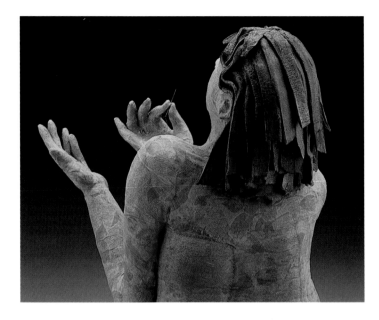

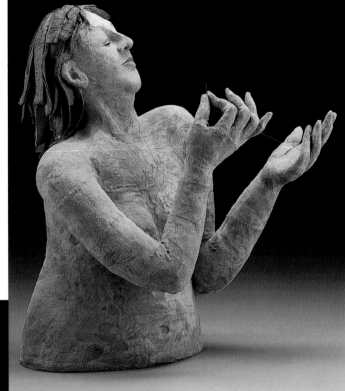

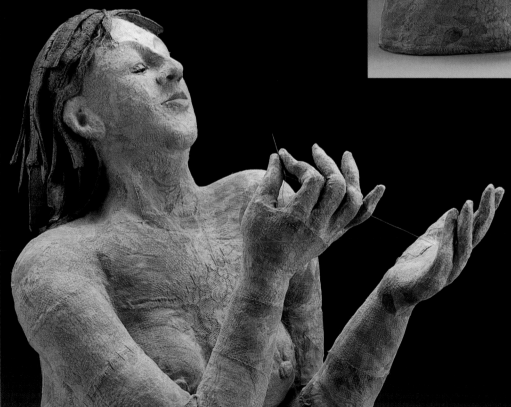

Photos: Bill Bachhuber

ARTIST: Leslie Lee
TITLE: More Mending
DIMENSIONS: 20" x 17" x 11"
MATERIALS/TECHNIQUES: Ceramic
with fabric

Roxie Ann Worthy

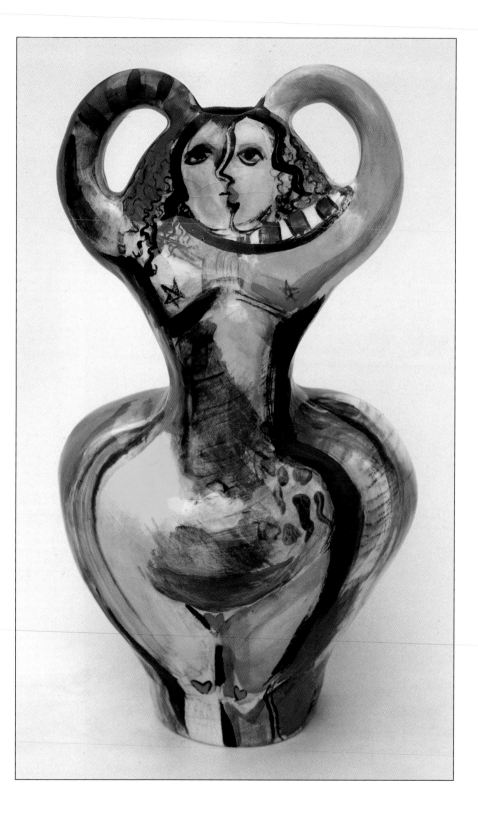

ARTIST: Roxie Ann Worthy
TITLE: Minoan Bull
DIMENSIONS: 18" x 10" x 8"
MATERIALS/TECHNIQUES: Earthenware, slabs, coils, underglaze, overglaze, lusters, china paints

Elise Sheridan Arnold

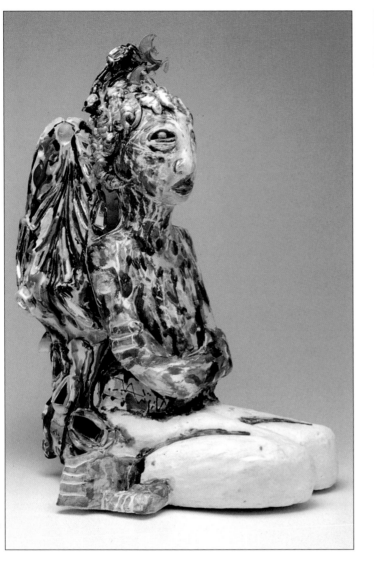

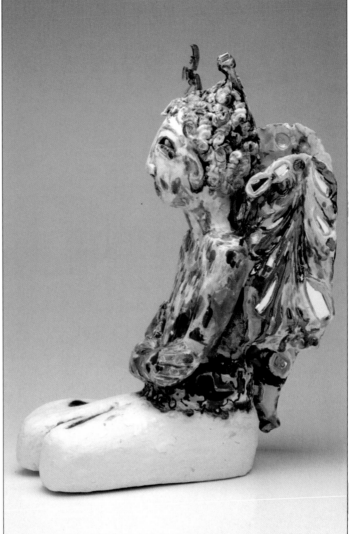

ARTIST: Elise Sheridan Arnold
TITLE: Temple Angel
DIMENSIONS: 23" x 17" x 13"
MATERIALS: Ceramics and glass

This piece was conceived from Arnold's
study of Oriental medicine and Eastern
philosophy, which embraces the idea of
one's own body being the most precious
temple that one dwells within.

Judith N. Condon

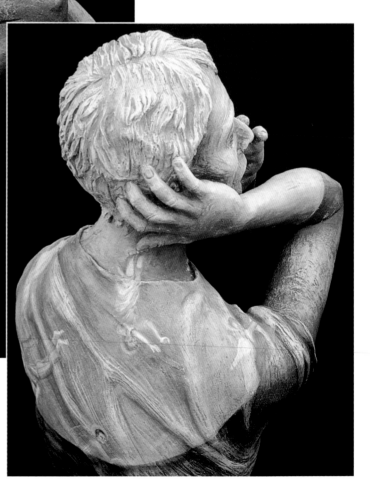

ARTIST: Judith N. Condon
TITLE: Male Figure with Angels
DIMENSIONS: 20" x 19" x 20"
MATERIALS/TECHNIQUES: Ceramic, slips,
oil paint

Jean Cappadonna-Nichols

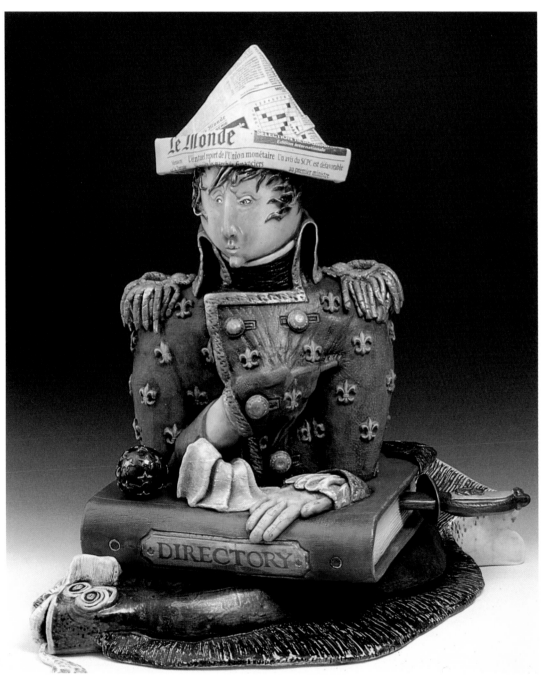

Photo: Bill Martin

ARTIST: Jean Cappadonna-Nichols
TITLE: Napoleon with Red Face and
Green Fish
DIMENSIONS: 34" x 38" x 27"
MATERIALS/TECHNIQUES: Whiteware,
glazes, stains, mixed media, hand built and
cast pieces

With this piece, Cappadonna-Nichols
creates one of her favorite persons in
history. She portrays Napoleon confronting
his "Waterloo," perched on a book of
(erroneous?) information, pistol under his
jacket, sitting on a long, green (rotting) fish.

Gary W. Benna

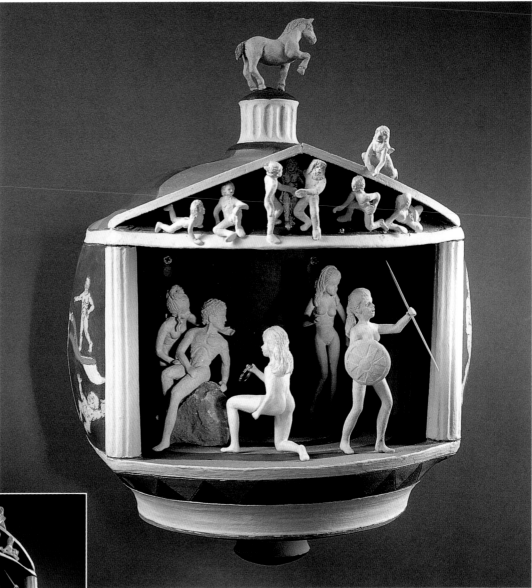

Photos: Robin Stancliff

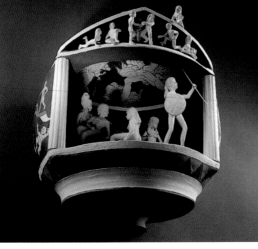

ARTIST: Gary W. Benna

TITLE: Judgement of Paris

DIMENSIONS: 18" x 15" x 12"

MATERIALS: Stoneware

TECHNIQUES: Thrown, with slab and press mold construction elements

Benna is intrigued by classical Greek mythology. His work marries the Greek myths to the simple elegant forms of Greek pottery, with its graceful drawings, and to Greek figurative sculptures.

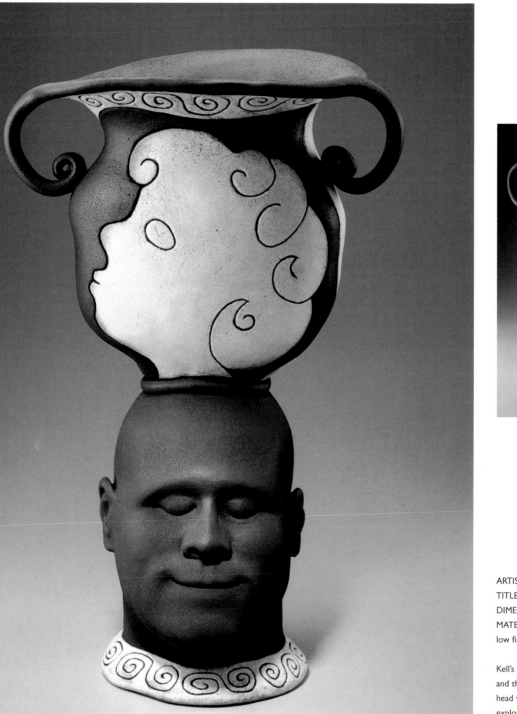

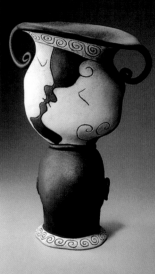

Photos: Andy Olenick

ARTIST: Jeff Kell
TITLE: Remembering
DIMENSIONS: 29" x 19" x 14"
MATERIALS/TECHNIQUES: Hand built, low fire

Kell's work explores human relationships and their accompanying emotions. The head vessel is a useful format for this exploration, as it provides a way of contrasting outward expression and inner thought.

Mary E. Williams

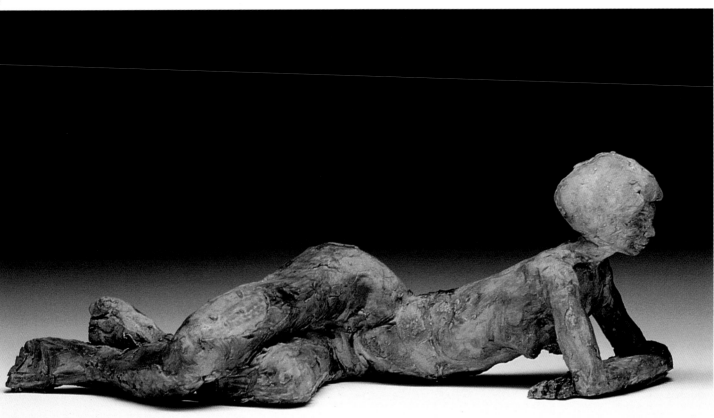

Photo: Philip J. Williams

ARTIST: Mary E. Williams
TITLE: Study In Repose II
DIMENSIONS: 14" x 7" x 5"
MATERIALS/TECHNIQUES: Clay

The female figure is the primary subject for
Williams' sculptures; she works in both clay
and stone.

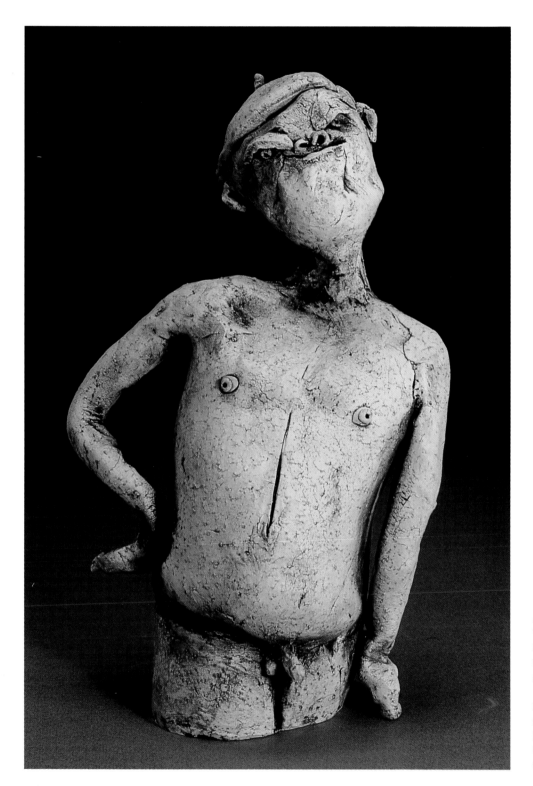

Caryn Marquardt

ARTIST: Caryn Marquardt
TITLE: Jake
DIMENSIONS: 3.5" x 4.5" x 10"
MATERIALS: White clay body containing sand

Marquardt's figures are not all human, but flow back and forth across the line between human and animal. By combining aspects of both, she uncovers a personality and reveals the psychological character of a piece.

Rod Moorhead

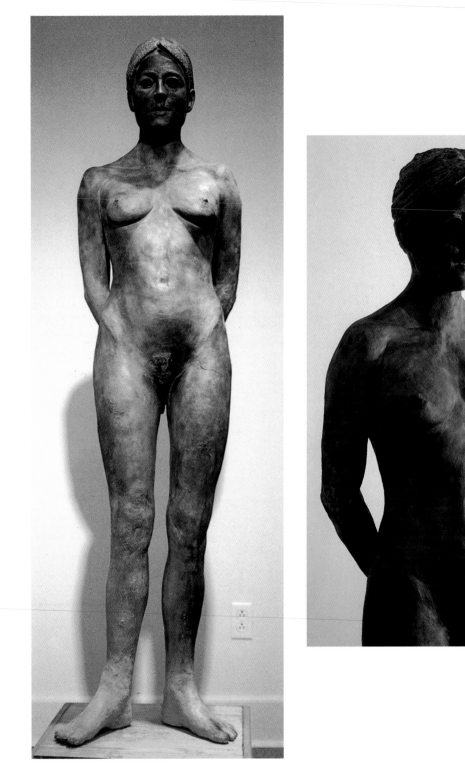

ARTIST: Rod Moorhead
TITLE: Bride
DIMENSIONS: 72" x 18" x 18"
MATERIALS/TECHNIQUES: Terra cotta,
pine base

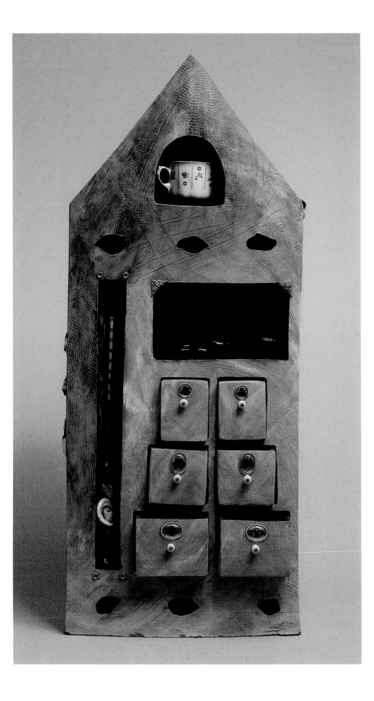

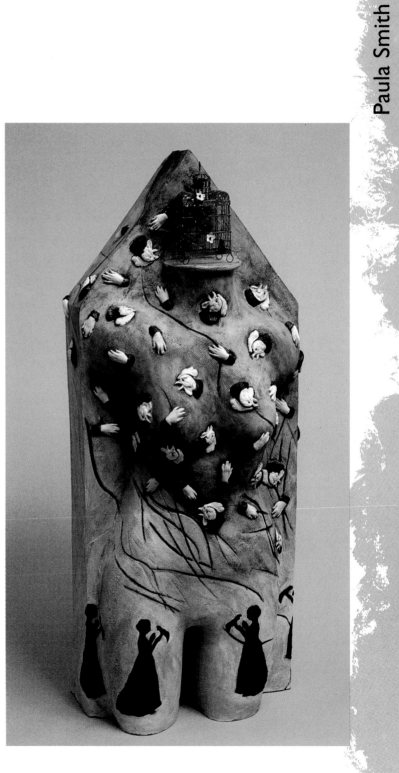

ARTIST: Paula Smith
TITLE: Common Keys
DIMENSIONS: 38" x 16" x 11"
MATERIALS/TECHNIQUES: Ceramics,
mixed

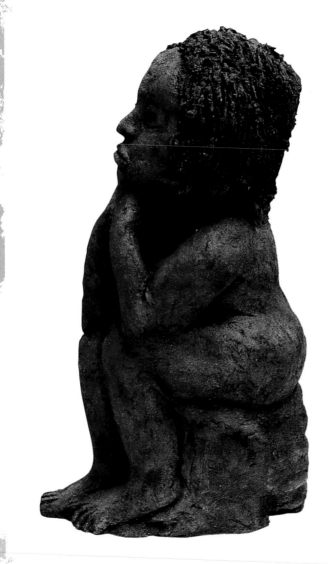

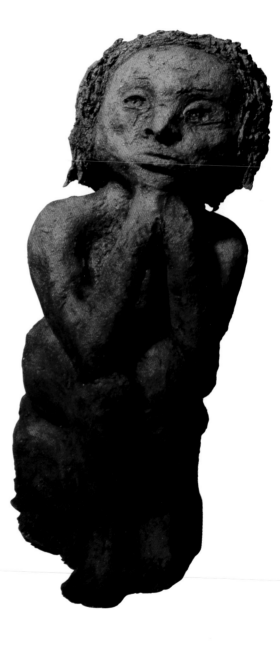

ARTIST: Elizabeth Featherstone Hoff
TITLE: Untitled
DIMENSIONS: 9" x 4" x 4.5"
MATERIALS: Stoneware, red iron oxide
TECHNIQUES: Hand built

Hoff likes people to bring their own stories
to her artwork, and through these stories,
define the work for themselves.

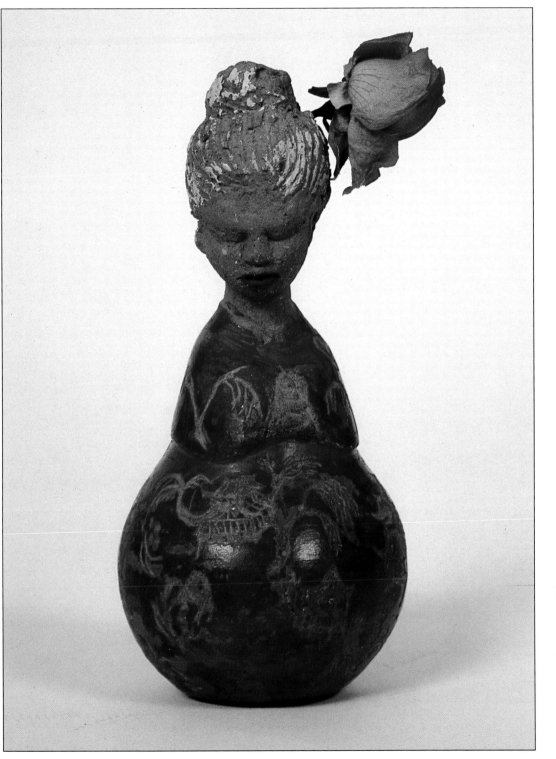

Hazel Mae Rotimi

ARTIST: Hazel Mae Rotimi
TITLE: Patience
DIMENSIONS: 6.75" x 3" x 3"
MATERIALS/TECHNIQUES: Local clay,
iron oxide, hand built, burnished, incised,
white clay slip

"Patience" is made from locally dug clay
and fired with cardboard strips in a trash
tin. Since studying in Nigeria, Howard has
sought new uses for low fired, unglazed
terra cottas.

Fleur E. Reynolds

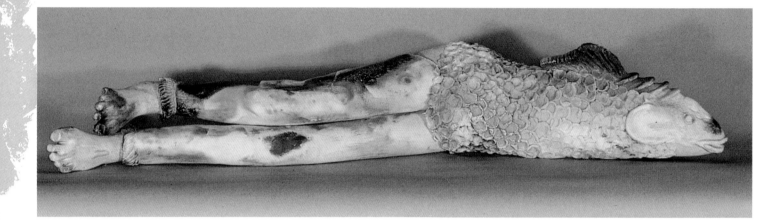

ARTIST: Fleur E. Reynolds
TITLE: Terra Pesche
DIMENSIONS: 12" x 48" x 7"
MATERIALS: Stoneware
TECHNIQUES: Slab construction, pit fired

Reynolds' ideas come from a variety of
sources, but most are a combination of
forms found in nature, or drawn from
mythology.

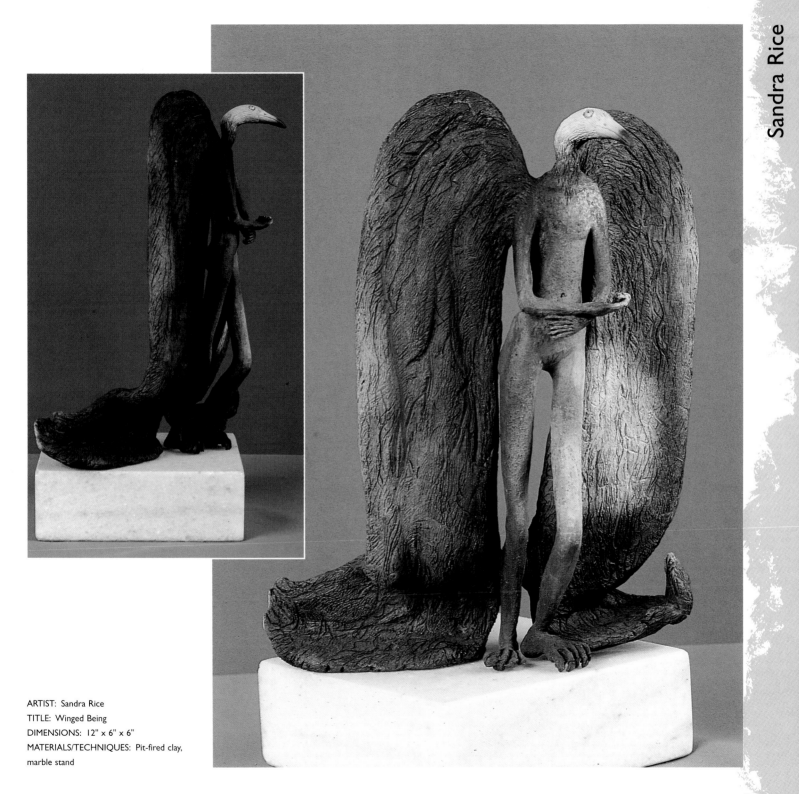

ARTIST: Sandra Rice
TITLE: Winged Being
DIMENSIONS: 12" x 6" x 6"
MATERIALS/TECHNIQUES: Pit-fired clay,
marble stand

Guangzhen "Poslin" Zhou

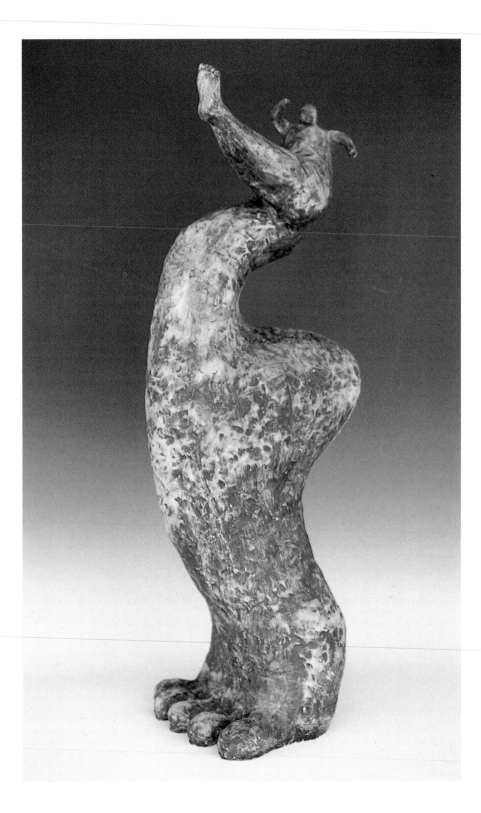

ARTIST: Guangzhen "Poslin" Zhou
TITLE: Kick Your xxx
DIMENSIONS: 31" x 10" x 11.5"
MATERIALS: Stoneware
TECHNIQUES: Hand built, black stains,
painted light blue acrylic color

In his feet series of sculptures, Zhou
creates the view of people through ant
eyes. The ant sees a giant foot, with a
smaller body up in the sky.

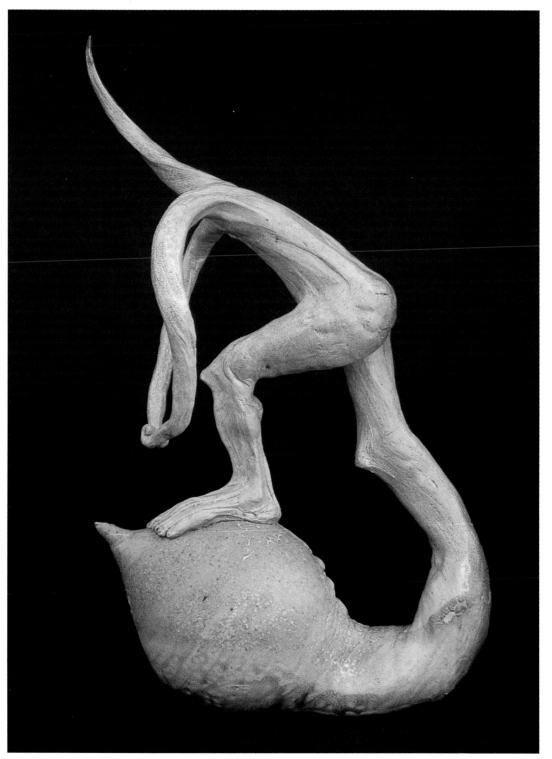

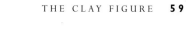

Samuel P. McCarty

ARTIST: Samuel P. McCarty
TITLE: Birth of Consciousness
DIMENSIONS: 18" x 10" x 10"
MATERIALS/TECHNIQUES: Stoneware,
salt fired

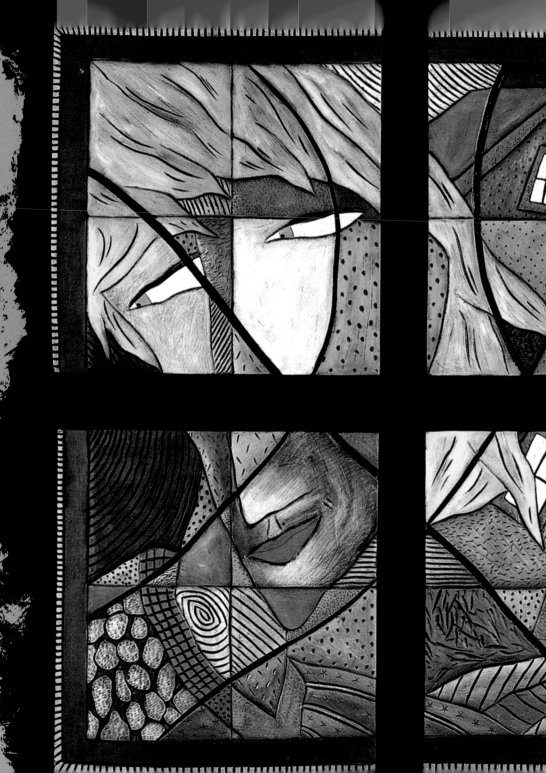

PAINTING, CARVING & RELIEFS

The act of painting on wet clay has a sensuality beyond that of charcoal or chalk on paper. In clay, lines have form and depth, there is a weight to the inscription. Gestural brushwork takes the surface from two to three dimensions. Somehow, like magic, the highest of art forms is fashioned from the natural materials of mud and water.

Sculpture represents and inhabits real space, but the two-dimensional medium of painting deals with space by implication alone. Ceramic artists have an added bonus with their medium; they use not only color, but also carving and low relief to create visual depth on a flat surface.

The appealing diversity of these pieces speaks to the range of styles of the artists: representational painting, abstract expressionist painting, figurative reliefs (as well as reliefs that hover between abstraction and representation), carved tile and painted tile. In each piece, the two-dimensional image interacts with the three-dimensional form in a way that helps the viewer realize the maker's sense of idea and content.

Several of the works have representational stories that take the narrative concept into the enigmatic, or imagery that deals with dreams and fantasies. They summon us to step into the story and contribute our own thoughts and feelings. Others of the wall-mounted pieces display a lavish interest in color and texture, richly executed but carefully composed. All have a strong physical presence, inviting each of us to be a participant in the art, not just an observer.

Beverlee Lehr

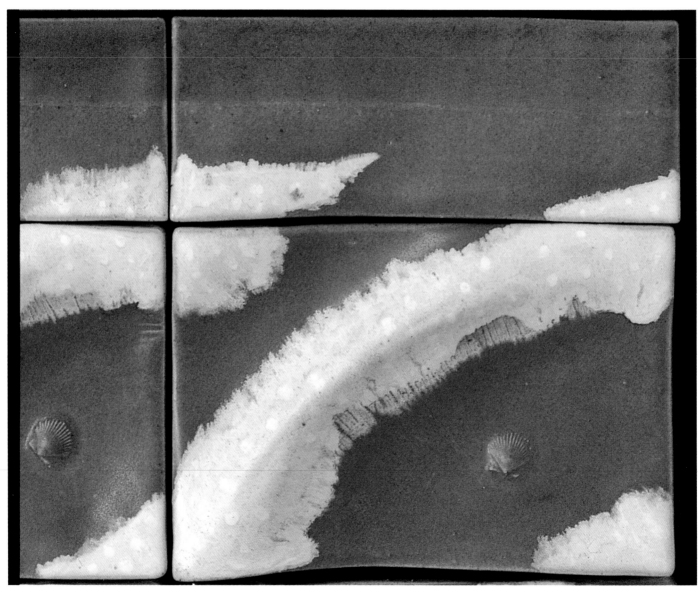

Photos: Socolow Photography

Beverlee Lehr

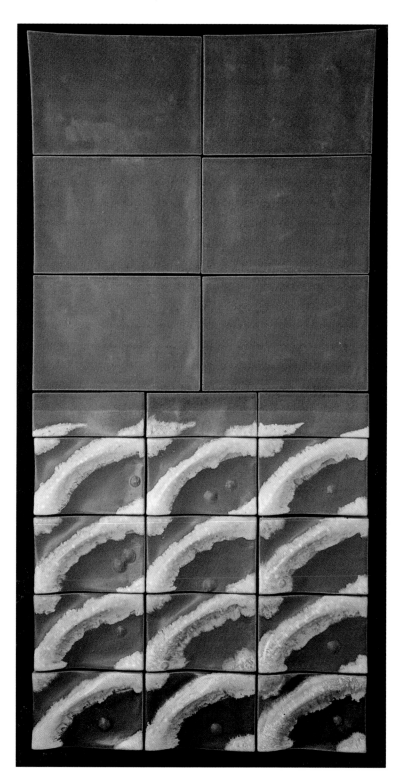

ARTIST: Beverlee Lehr
TITLE: Blue Horizon: Sanibel Island
DIMENSIONS: 55" x 27" x 3"
MATERIALS/TECHNIQUES: Hand built
stoneware
OPPOSITE PAGE: Detail

Lehr works with visual memories of
landscapes, plants and human anatomy.
She focuses on the expressive use of
colored glazes and the jewel-like quality
of glazed surfaces. This piece was
inspired by a walk on the beach in Florida.

Diane O'Grady

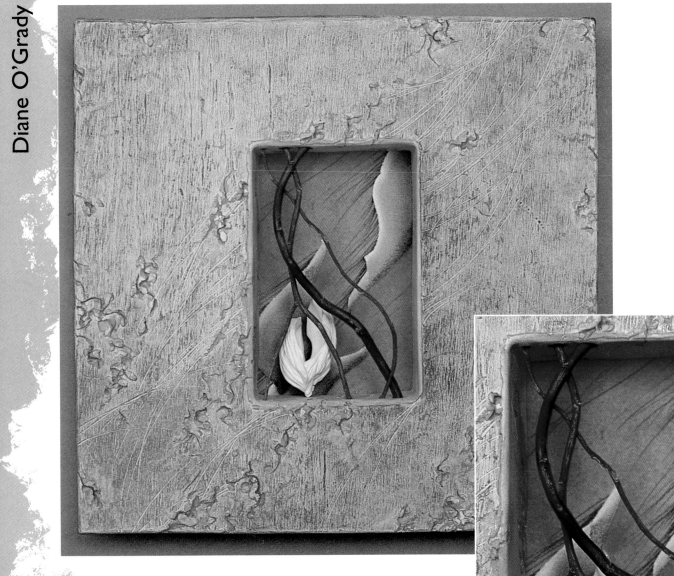

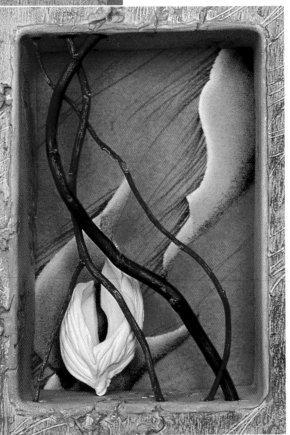

ARTIST: Diane O'Grady
TITLE: Untitled
DIMENSIONS: 11.5" x 12" x 1.875"
MATERIALS/TECHNIQUES: Porcelain,
pastel on paper, willow branches

O'Grady combines aspects of the natural
environment with elements of the built
environment. This piece is about growth —
intellectural growth, spiritual growth, but
also the literal growth in nature.

Susanne G. Stephenson

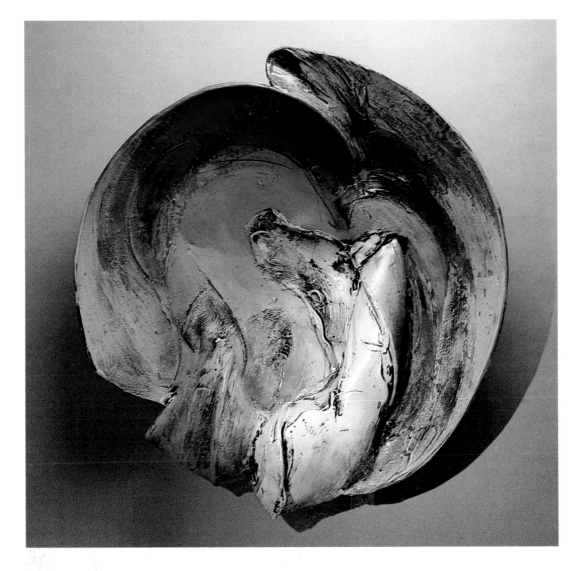

ARTIST: Susanne G. Stephenson
TITLE: Dusk V
DIMENSIONS: 29" x 27" x 8"
MATERIALS/TECHNIQUES: Terra cotta, thrown and constucted, color clay slips thickly applied by hand and brush

The focus of Stephenson's work is abstracting landscapes in low-fire terra cotta clay. She does not record the geography of a scene, but rather the mood or visual energy of nature at a particular time.

Amy M. Nelson

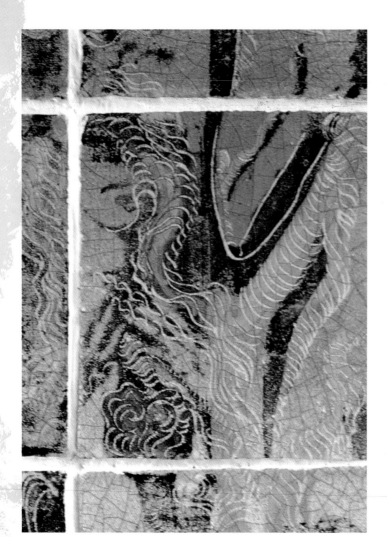

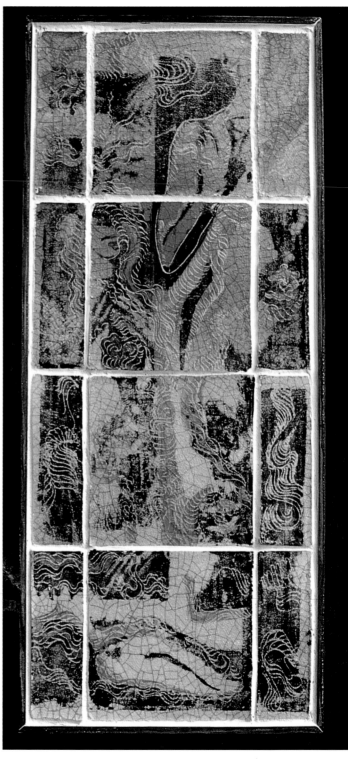

ARTIST: Amy M. Nelson

TITLE: Woman as Icon

DIMENSIONS: 21" x 9" x 1"

MATERIALS/TECHNIQUES: Ceramic tile
with silkscreen manipulation

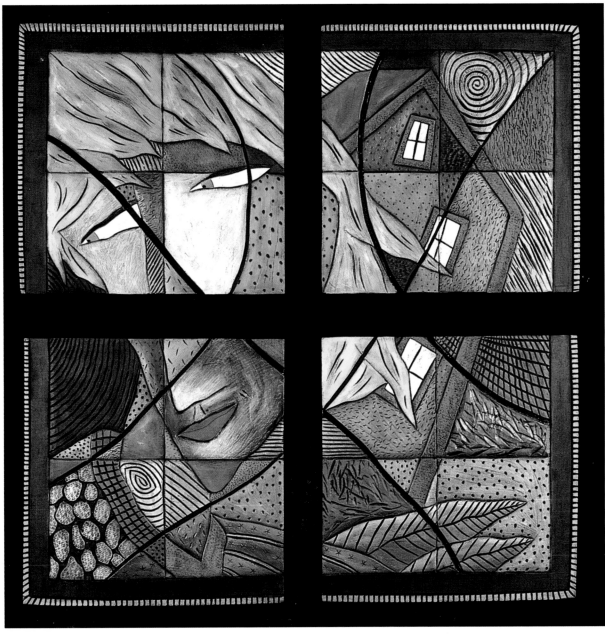

Photo: Mark Amerman

ARTIST: David Stabley
TITLE: Wall Tile Composition
DIMENSIONS: 32" x 32" x .5"
MATERIALS: Slab-constructed red
earthenware
TECHNIQUES: Drawn and carved,
decorated with acrylics and a wax/oil patina

Stabley's work is based on ideas about
dreams, and how we remember dreams in
fragmented ways. He explores space, texture,
surface and the overlapping of objects to
create this sense of fragmentation.

Judith Decker-Sylva

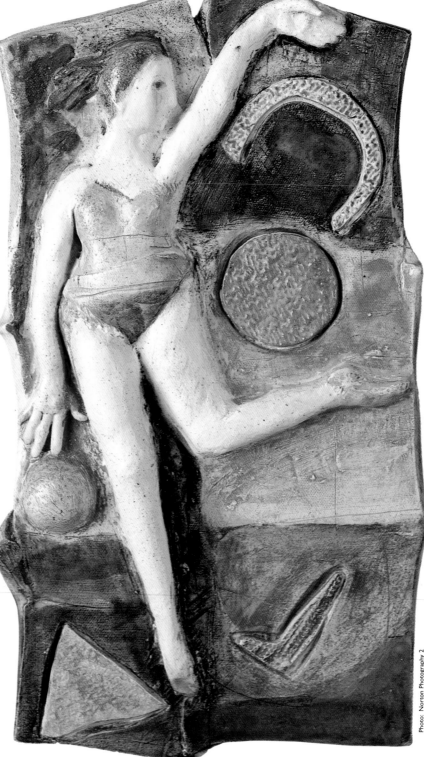

ARTIST: Judith Decker-Sylva
TITLE: Game Player
DIMENSIONS: 14.5" x 8"
MATERIALS/TECHNIQUES: White
stoneware, colored with stains and glazes,
oxidation fired

Decker-Sylva has a background in painting
and drawing, which becomes evident in her
three-dimensional relief work.

Elizabeth MacDonald

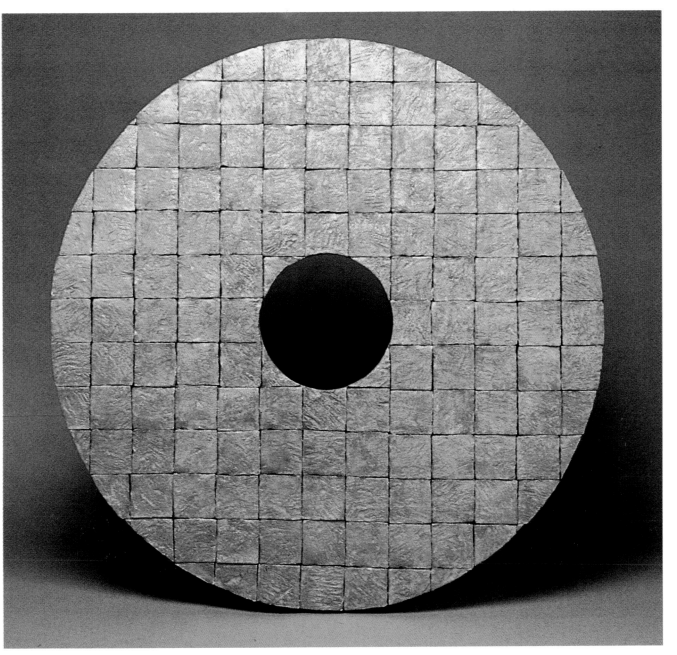

Photo: Joseph Kugelsky

ARTIST: Elizabeth MacDonald
TITLE: Gold Wheel with Tiles
DIMENSIONS: 43" x 43" x 2"
MATERIALS/TECHNIQUES: Clay

Pamela Mahaffey

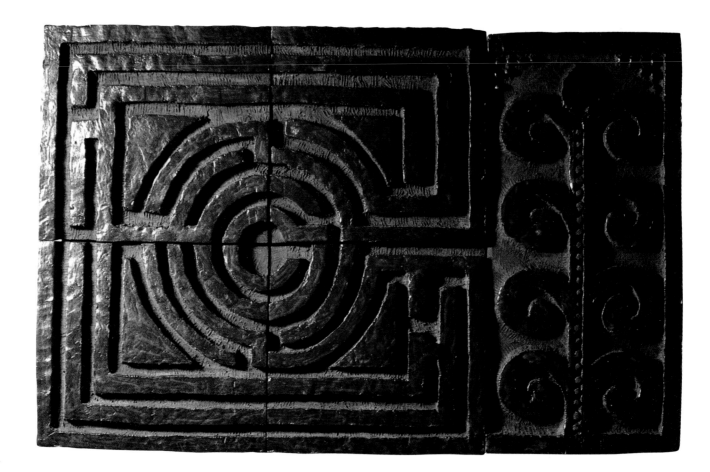

ARTIST: Pamela Mahaffey
TITLE: Labyrinth
DIMENSIONS: 16.25" x 25.5" x 2.5"
MATERIALS/TECHNIQUES: Stoneware,
cobalt and maganese oxides

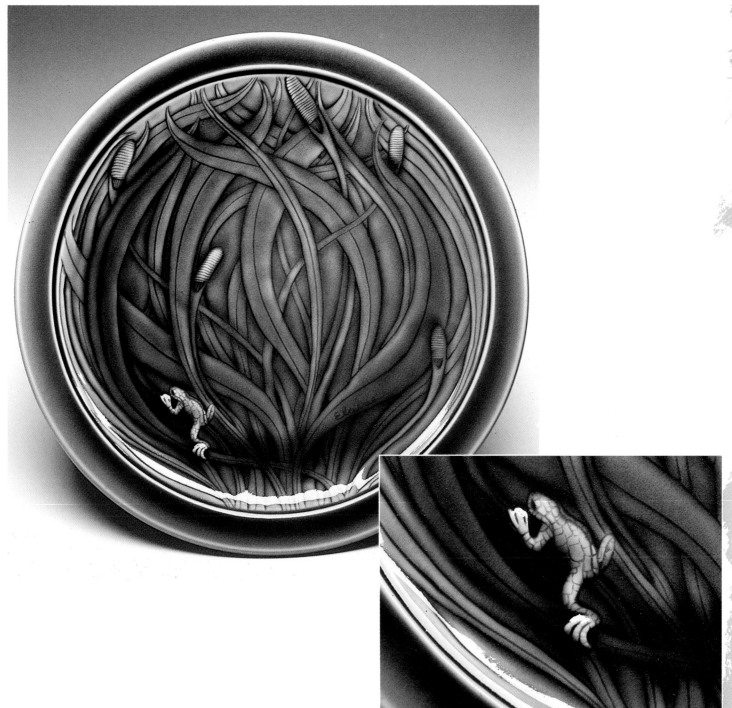

ARTIST: Elaine Coleman
TITLE: Incised Porcelain Frog Plate
DIMENSIONS: 14" x 1.5"

Marilyn Lysohir

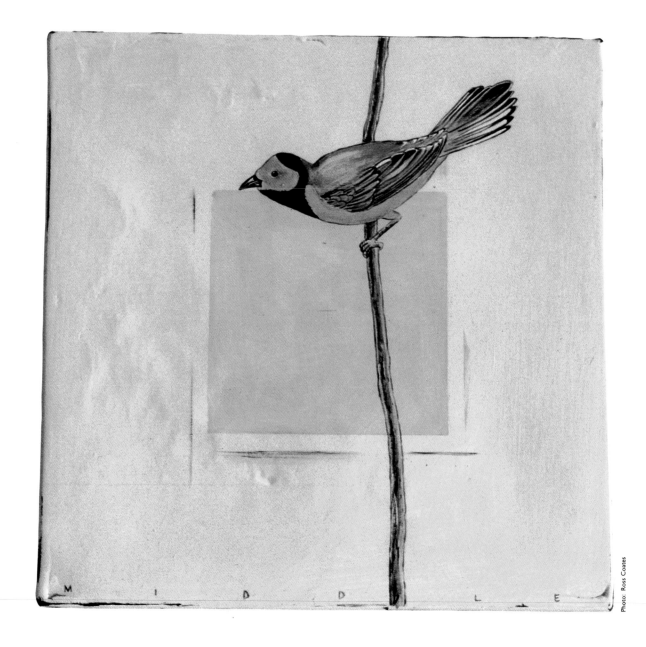

Photo: Ross Coates

Marilyn Lysohir

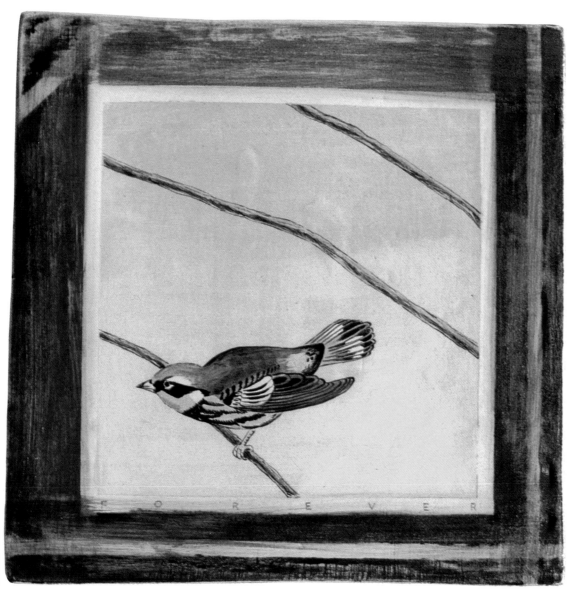

Photo: Ross Coates

ARTIST: Marilyn Lysohir
TITLE: The Tattooed Ladies and the
Dinosaurs (2 of 90 tiles)
DIMENSIONS: 12" x 12" x .5" each
MATERIALS/TECHNIQUES: Low-fire
underglazed tile

"The Tattooed Ladies and the Dinosaurs"
is a large ceramic installation that will have
over 1,000 hand made dinosaur bones, 90
glazed tiles and two life-sized tattooed
women walking through the field of bones.
The tiles showing birds will be a backdrop
for a piece performed by The Pat Graney
Dance Company in Seattle.

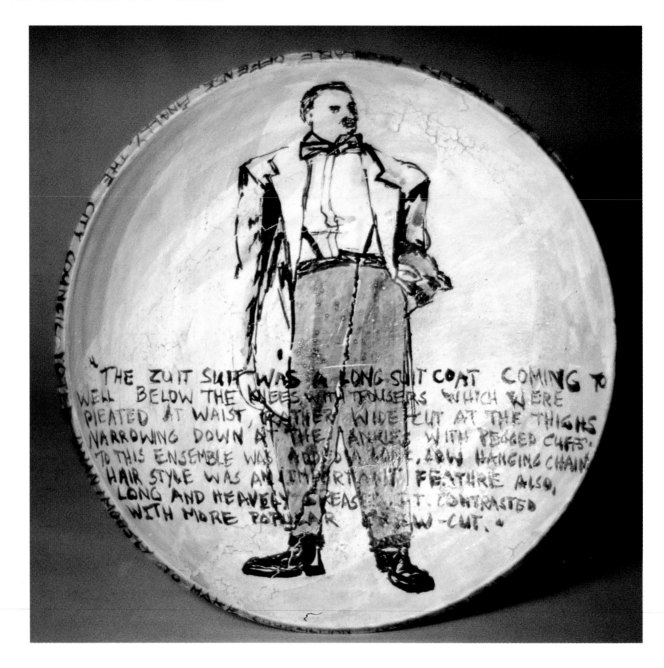

ARTIST: Terri Hughes

TITLE: Zoot Suite Riots

DIMENSIONS: 18" x 18" x 4"

MATERIALS/TECHNIQUES: Clay, slips, oxides, low-fire glazes

Hughes' recent works are about the search for truth, knowledge and critical thinking. "My art work speaks about how I was educated and 'fed' information. It questions the perspective from which I was taught, and what I wasn't taught. Why was I so naive about other cultures? Why didn't I even ponder racial and social injustice in the United States?"

Jerry L. Caplan

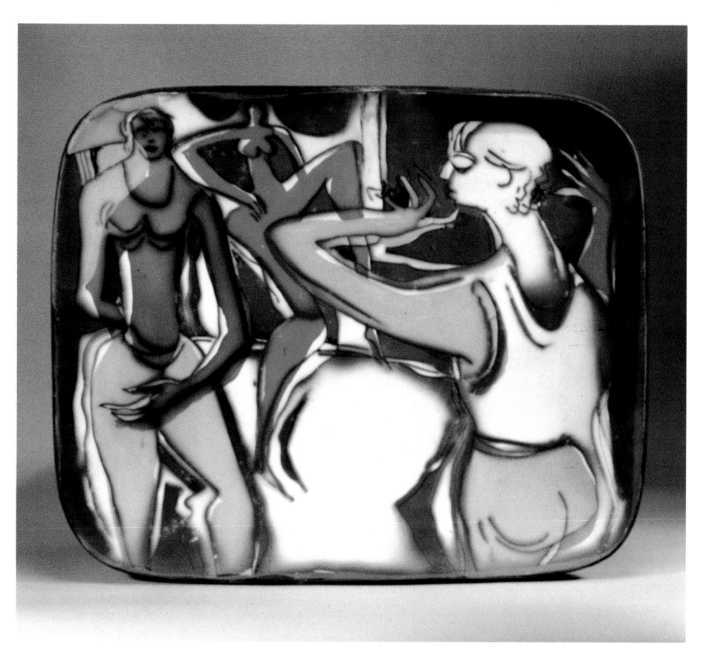

ARTIST: Jerry L. Caplan
TITLE: Rehearsal
DIMENSIONS: 13" x 14" x 2"
MATERIALS/TECHNIQUES: Low-fire raku,
reduction stenciling

Julie Tesser

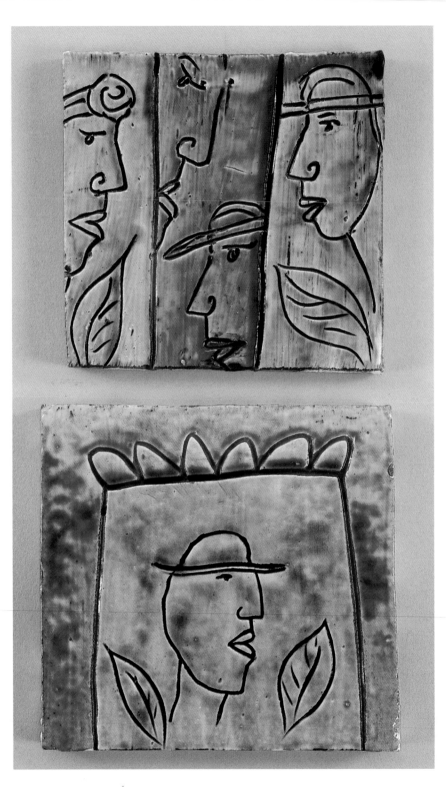

ARTIST: Julie Tesser

TITLE: Untitled

DIMENSIONS: top 7" x 7" x .75"

bottom 7.5" x 8" x .75"

MATERIALS/TECHNIQUES: Terra cotta,

sgraffito

Tesser's tiles are spontaneous and personal drawings that express thoughts about people and their relationships in life. They are symbols respresenting the ideas of a culture, the family and the home.

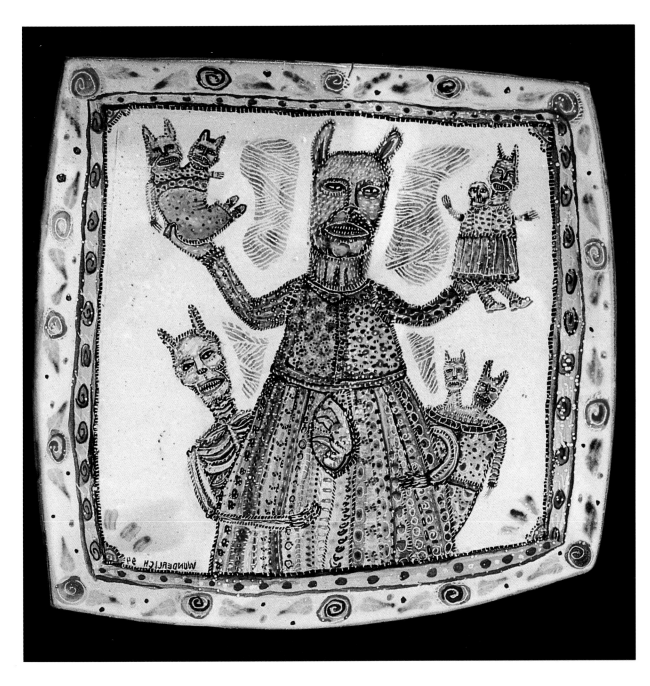

ARTIST: Janis Mars Wunderlich

TITLE: My Guardian

DIMENSIONS: 10" x 10.5"

MATERIALS/TECHNIQUES: Terra cotta, majolica glaze, slab, tile

Wunderlich's sculptures speak of passages and coming of age. The two-headed figure symbolizes the precarious yet vital balance of the interior (soul) and the exterior (body). Intricately detailed dresses and carefully buckled shoes suggest the innocent era of childhood, while the masked faces remind us of adulthood.

Julia Putman

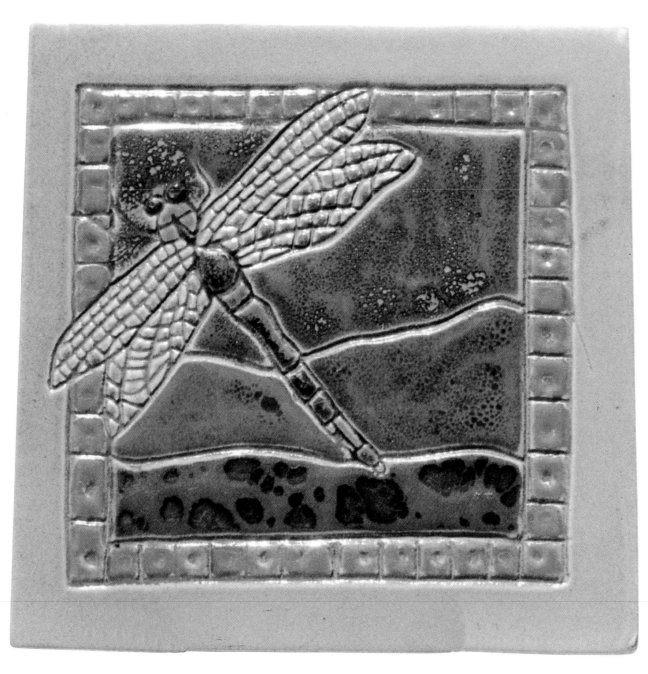

ARTIST: Julia Putnam

TITLE: Summertime Dragonfly

DIMENSIONS: 6" x 6"

MATERIALS/TECHNIQUES: Maganese clay, white slip applied and carved, hand painted with stoneware glazes

Alena Ort

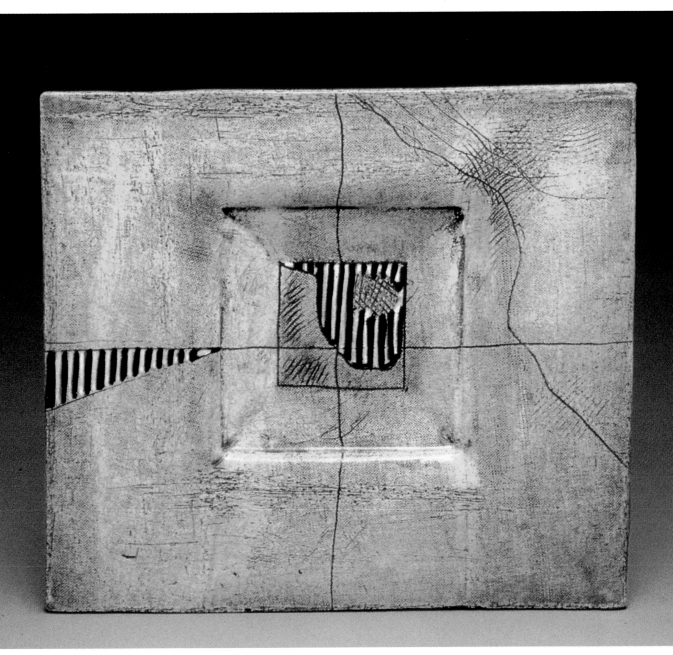

Photo: Theresa Schmiendt

ARTIST: Alena Ort
TITLE: Abstract Landscape
DIMENSIONS: 9" x 9" x .5"
MATERIALS/TECHNIQUES: Stoneware,
oxides, hand built, low fire

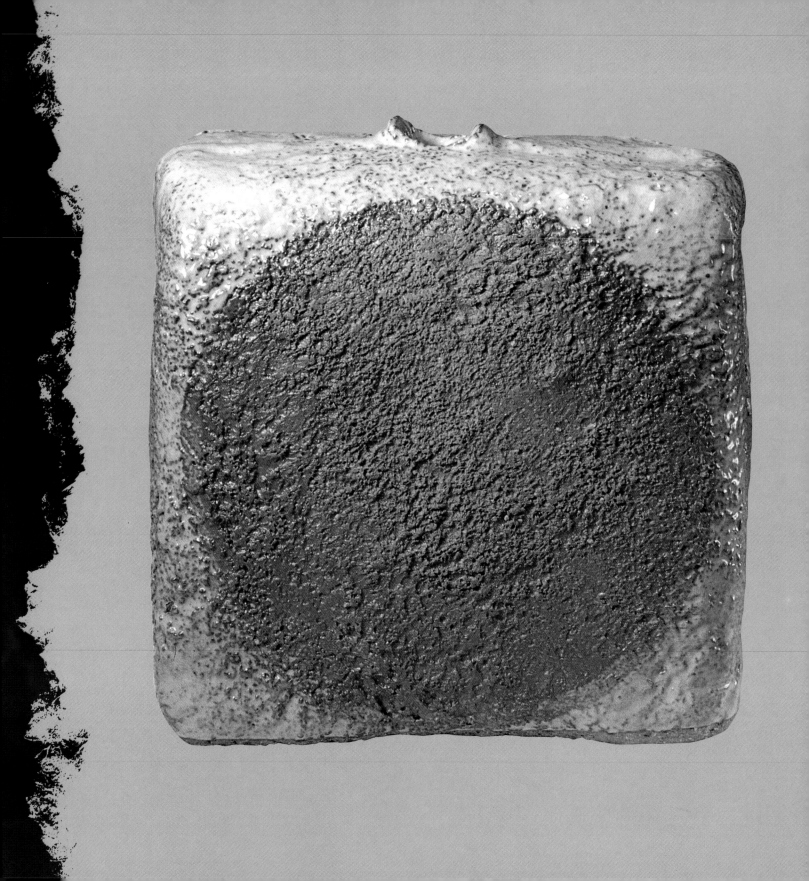

VESSEL 81 FORMS

"'Tis the gift to be simple, 'tis the gift to be free . . ." goes the line from the old Shaker song. These words might be used to describe the ceramic vessel, that enigmatic form that is simplicity itself, yet requires enormous skills, discipline and perseverance to get just right.

The vessel, our earliest art form, is still, today, the heart of ceramic art — the form that ceramic artists return to again and again. Open container forms, whether tall cylindrical vessels and jars or low spreading bowls, carry a memory of all the pots of civilization. The best vessels also take on an individual identity and contribute to the tradition.

These award-winning artists explore a wide range of possibilities based on both hand built and wheel-thrown hollow forms, with diverse approaches to design and decoration. Interior surfaces evoke private places; even the rims invite investigation. Pattern and texture interact with glazes and firing marks to translate the artist's idea into tangible form.

But look beyond the surface treatment to the vessel's subtle contours. Even the familiar shapes are rich with references and display the spontaneous marks of the maker. Some are quiet and functional; others say more about form and less about function. Equally often the function is no function at all, other than to provide a visual experience.

Because they possess an intensity of feeling, these vessels have substance well beyond the ordinary, a formal sculptural presence. And one knows that their makers have developed a fond rapport with their materials, rather than a victory over them.

Hiroshi Nakayama

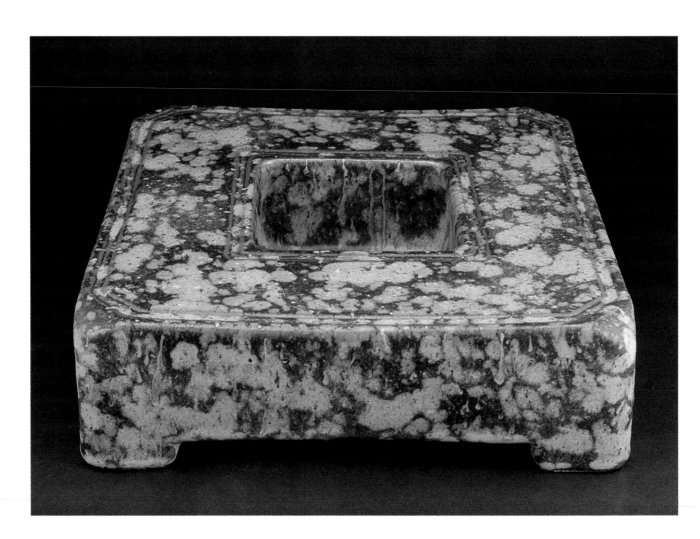

ARTIST: Hiroshi Nakayama

TITLE: Ceremonial Vessel

DIMENSIONS: 3.25" x 11.375" x 11.375"

MATERIALS: High-fire stoneware, wood ash glazes

TECHNIQUES: A combination of wheel thrown and slab built

Nakayama has developed a wood ash glaze that has the appearance and feel of polished stone. The surface is so integrated with the clay form that they appear to be made out of one solid material.

Kate Inskeep

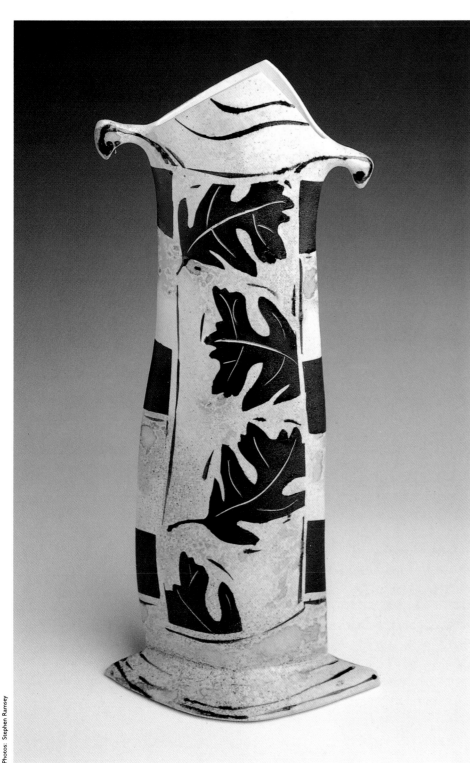

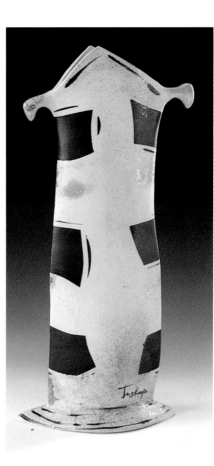

ARTIST: Kate Inskeep
TITLE: Tall Oak Vase
DIMENSIONS: 16" x 8" x 4"
MATERIALS: Porcelain, black slip, soda and
volcanic ash glaze
TECHNIQUES: Hand built

Inskeep is interested in the animation of
form and how the use of decoration can
accentuate the movement of a form. She
uses stencils to apply the black slip decoration; this achieves the crisp, sharp lines
reminiscent of wood block prints.

Photos: Stephen Ramsey

Guadalupe Lanning Robinson

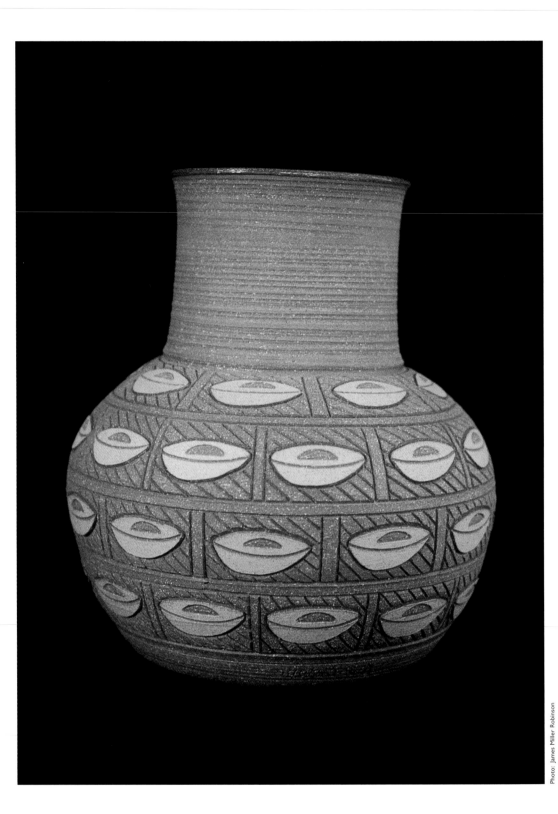

ARTIST: Guadalupe Lanning Robinson
TITLE: Avocados
DIMENSIONS: 12.5" x 12" x 12"
MATERIALS/TECHNIQUES: Incised
stoneware

Photo: James Miller Robinson

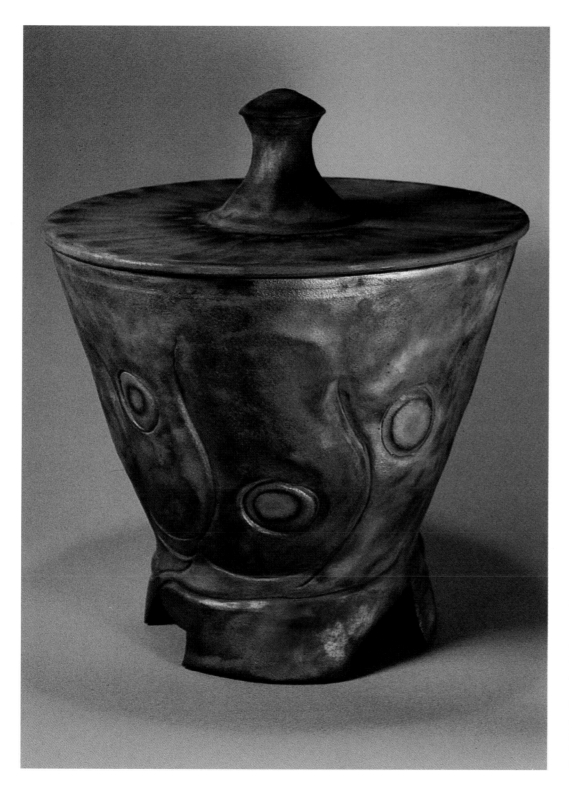

Tobias Weissman

ARTIST: Tobias Weissman
TITLE: Many Faces
DIMENSIONS: 16"
MATERIALS/TECHNIQUES: Raku, wheel
thrown, altered and carved, torched in
sections to create blue copper finish

Weissman creates strong, stable forms
that emit a sense of security and well-being.
He strives to give the viewer a sense of
imaginative and suggestive power, as well
as peace, harmony and balance.

Susan A. Beecher

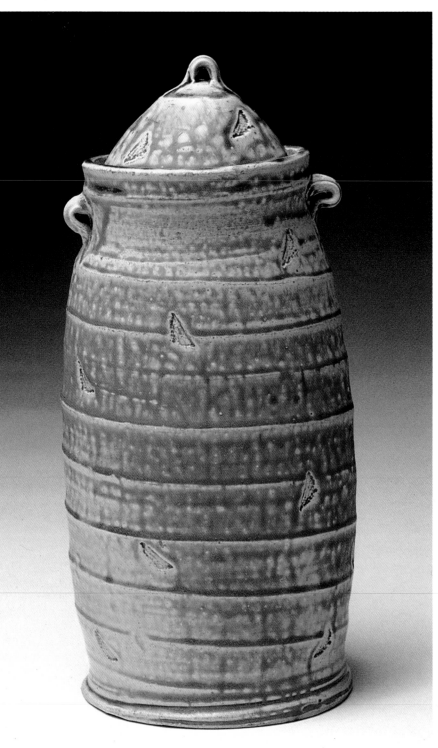

ARTIST: Susan A. Beecher
TITLE: Oval Jar
DIMENSIONS: 11" x 5" x 4"
MATERIALS: White stoneware
TECHNIQUES: High-fired in wood and
salt, wood ash glaze

Photo: D. James Dee

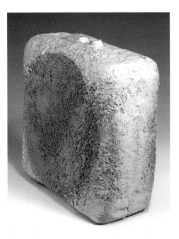

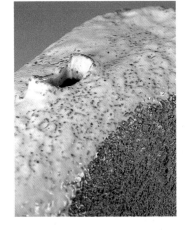

Robin Johnson

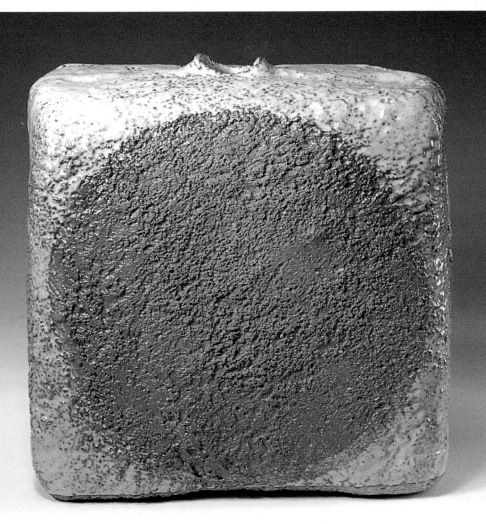

ARTIST: Robin Johnson
TITLE: Homage to Scully
DIMENSIONS: 10" x 10" x 4.5"
MATERIALS: Stoneware, shino glaze
TECHNIQUES: Hand built

This piece was inspired by Vincent Scully,
and a quote from Scully's book, *Architecture:
The Natural and the Manmade* (p. 117):
" . . . the human body is favored by being so
proportioned that it can fit into the perfect
shapes of square and circle, which are by
implication those that reveal the basic
order of the universe."

Lee Akins

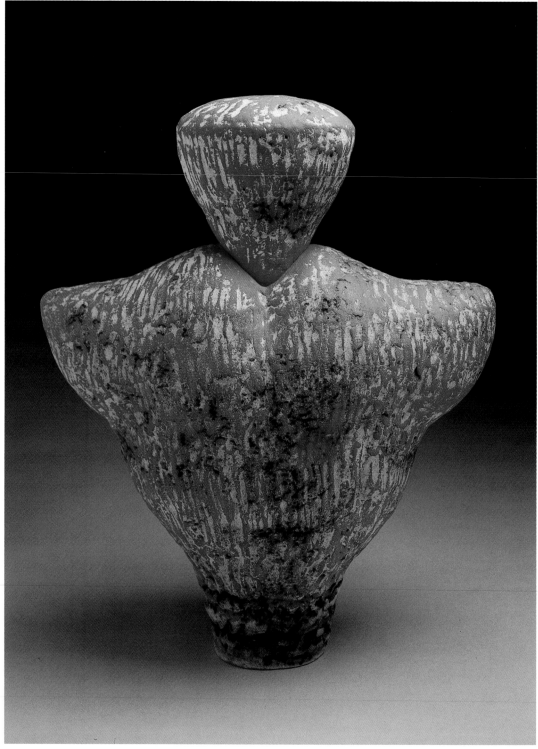

ARTIST: Lee Akins
TITLE: Lidded Torso Bottle
DIMENSIONS: 17" x 14" x 7"
MATERIALS: Terra cotta
TECHNIQUES: Coil built

Akins' work seeks to combine figurative
imagery with the format of the traditional
clay vessel. The vessel is a powerful
metaphor for the body, with each part of
the pot being named for a corresponding
area of the body. A full lip, a gentle curve
of the neck, a rotund belly or a broad
shoulder — these elements combine to
animate the vessel.

Yoshiro Ikeda

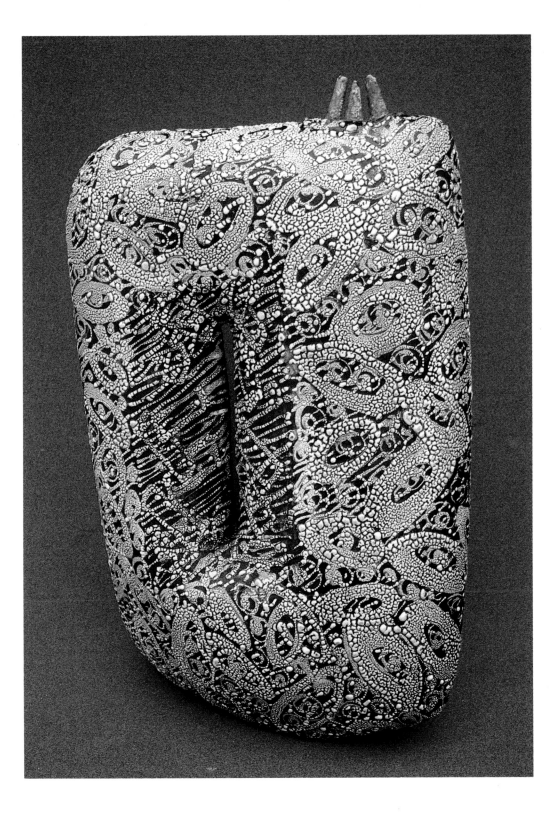

ARTIST: Yoshiro Ikeda
TITLE: Winter
DIMENSIONS: 27" x 15" x 7"
MATERIALS/TECHNIQUES: Clay, coil built

Cynthia Bringle

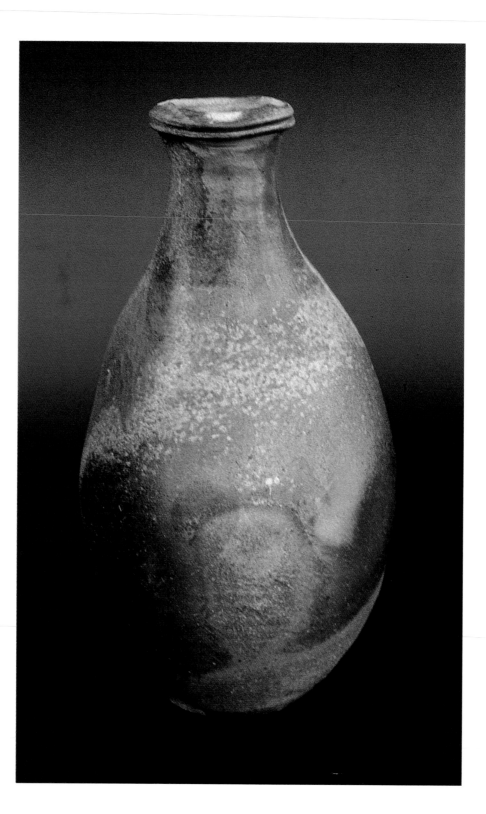

ARTIST: Cynthia Bringle
TITLE: Oval Vase
DIMENSIONS: 16" x 9" x 8"
MATERIALS/TECHNIQUES: Clay, wheel
thrown, coil, altered, wood fired

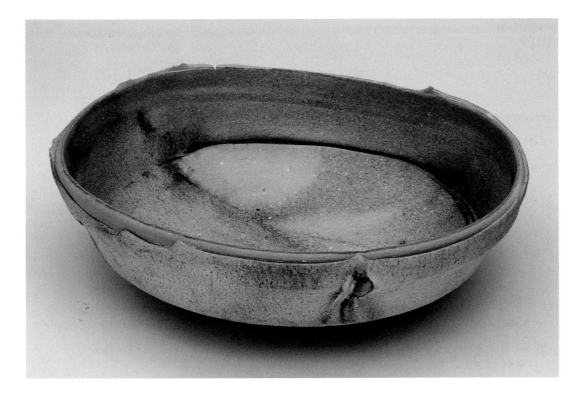

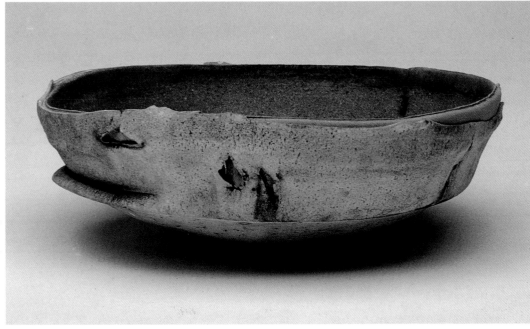

Photos: Eve Vandernett & John Buffington

ARTIST: Karl Yost
TITLE: Bowl
DIMENSIONS: 11" x 11" x 5"
MATERIALS: Stoneware, glazes, slips
TECHNIQUES: Wheel thrown

This piece is one in a series of landscape studies completed after a journey to Colorado.

Jan Schachter

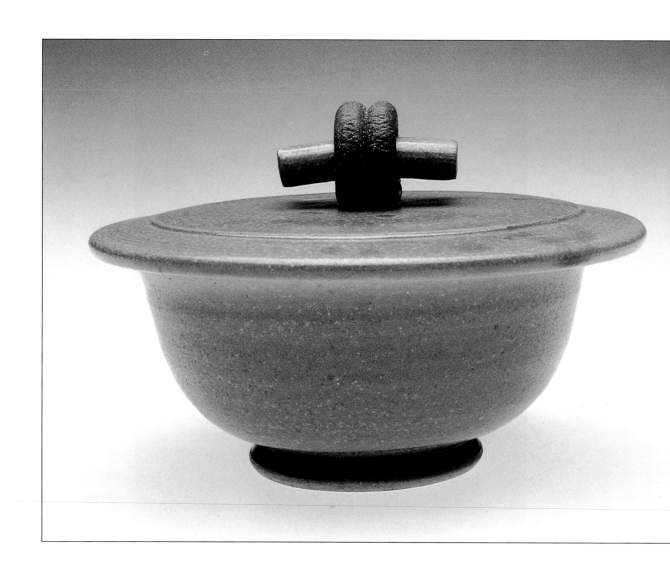

Photo: Ira Schrank

ARTIST: Jan Schachter
TITLE: Covered Bowl
DIMENSIONS: 3.75" x 6" x 6"
MATERIALS/TECHNIQUES: Stoneware,
reduction

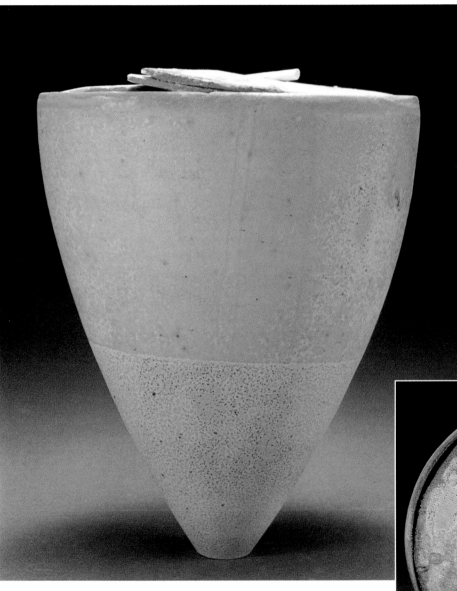

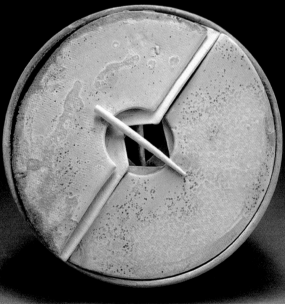

ARTIST: G. E. Colpitts
TITLE: Vessel Form #51
DIMENSIONS: 4.875" x 4" x 4"
MATERIALS/TECHNIQUES: Porcelain,
thrown, hand built, lithium glaze

Posey Bacopoulos

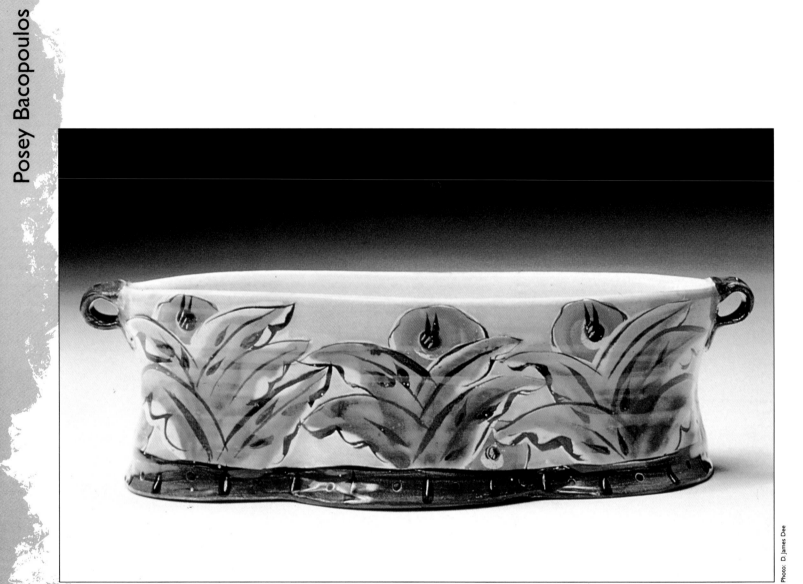

Photo: D. James Dee

ARTIST: Posey Bacopoulos

TITLE: Oval Server

DIMENSIONS: 4" x 13" x 4.5"

MATERIALS/TECHNIQUES: Majolica on
terra cotta

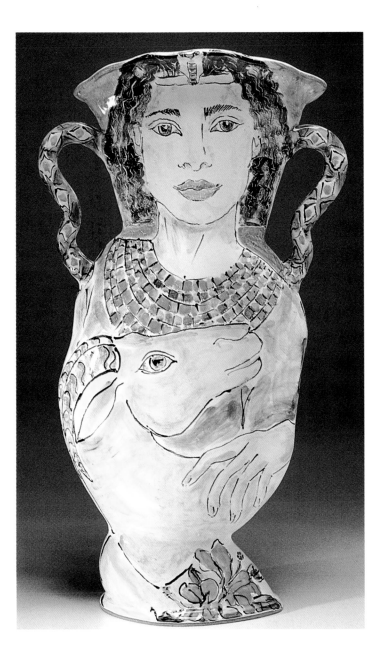

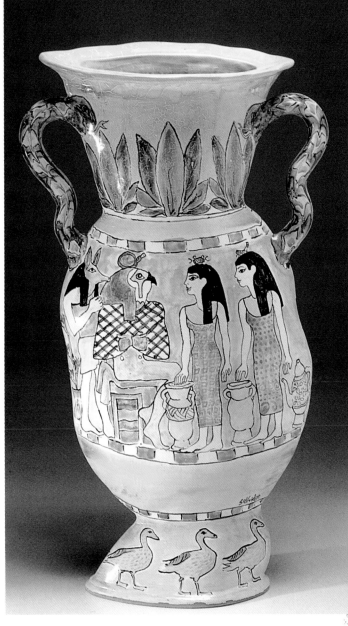

Carol & Richard Selfridge

ARTISTS: Carol and Richard Selfridge
TITLE: Selket, Goddess of Magic or
The Girls Sell Our Work at Sotheby's
DIMENSIONS: 28.5" x 16.5" x 7"
MATERIALS/TECHNIQUES: Majolica-
glazed terra cotta, constructed

The Selfridges use press-molded elements
which are cut, altered, stacked and joined.
They like the way the large, illusionistic
pieces in this series look like a pot in a
painting by Matisse or Braque or Picasso.

Ron Shady

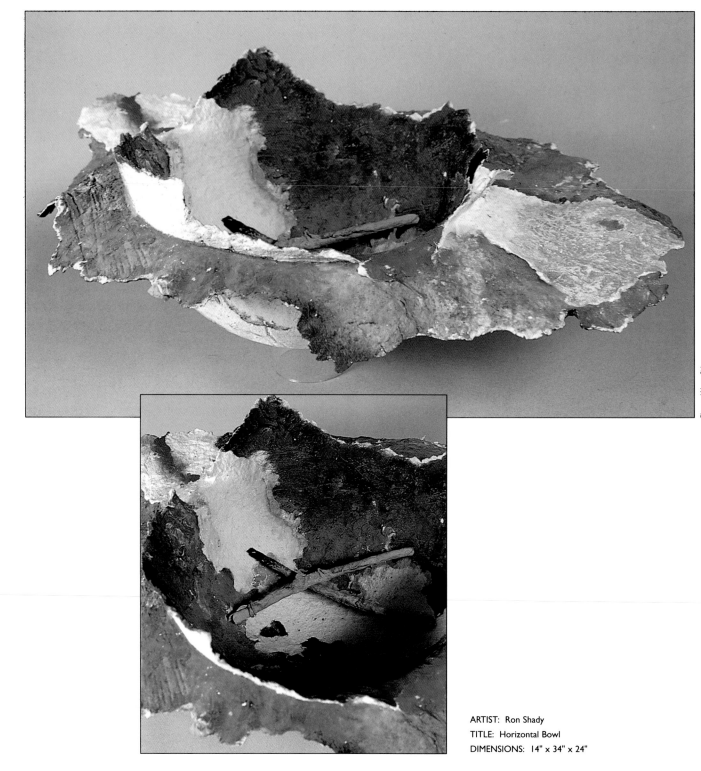

Photos: Wayne Sides

ARTIST: Ron Shady
TITLE: Horizontal Bowl
DIMENSIONS: 14" x 34" x 24"

Nancy Heller

Photo: Sharon Goodman

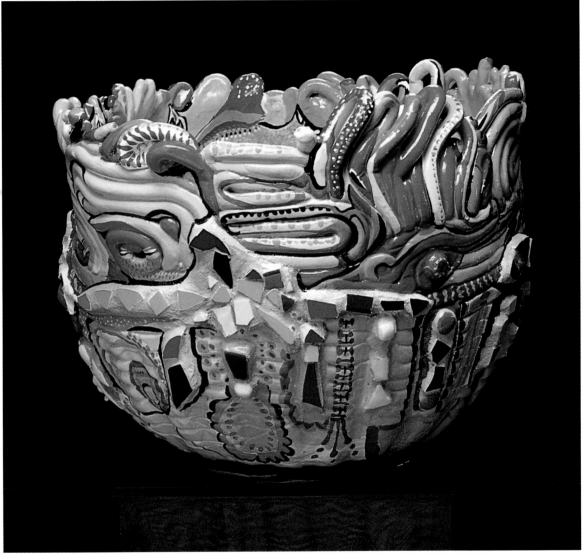

ARTIST: Nancy Heller

TITLE: Ceramic Planter

DIMENSIONS: 16" x 14" x 16"

MATERIALS/TECHNIQUES: Extruded coils

of clay, mirror and clay fragments

Richey Bellinger

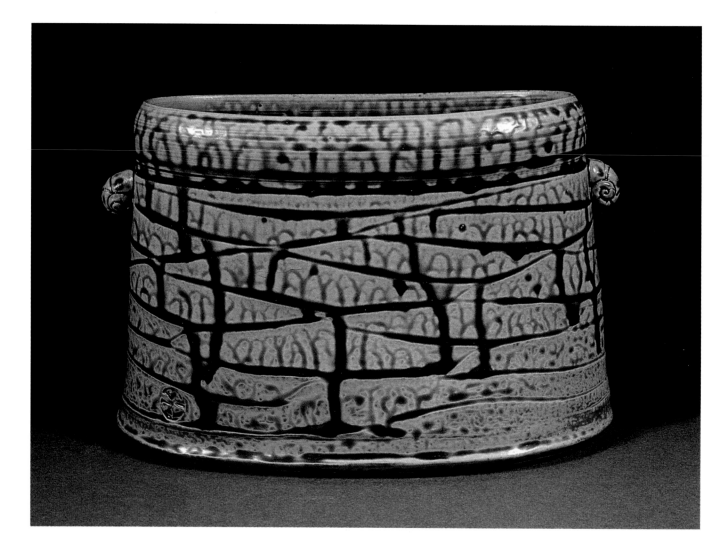

ARTIST: Richey Bellinger
TITLE: Oval Vessel
DIMENSIONS: 6" x 9" x 5"
MATERIALS/TECHNIQUES: Porcelain

Bellinger finds inspiration in such things as
the patterns and grain found in wood and
rocks, the blend of color in the sky at dusk,
and the effect of looking a long way out
over the ocean.

Rex Fogt

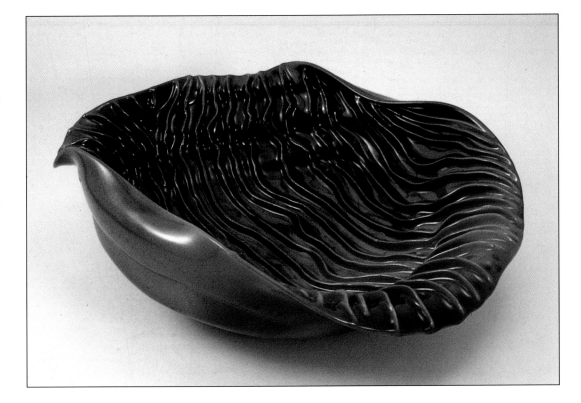

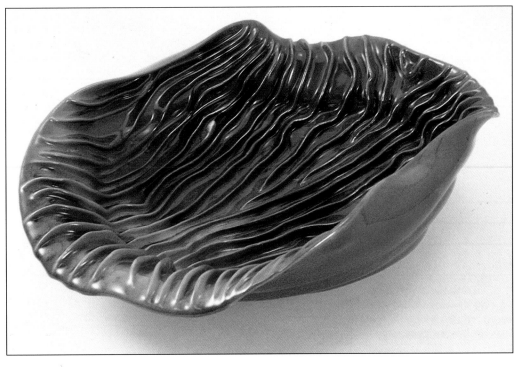

ARTIST: Rex Fogt
TITLE: Slurpie Flow
DIMENSIONS: 6" x 13" x 17"
MATERIALS: Porcelain
TECHNIQUES: This piece is glazed with
a high fire. (Most lusters are produced at
lower temperatures.) Luster producing
materials are put into the raw glaze, and
applied to the bisque porcelain.

C. Keen Zero

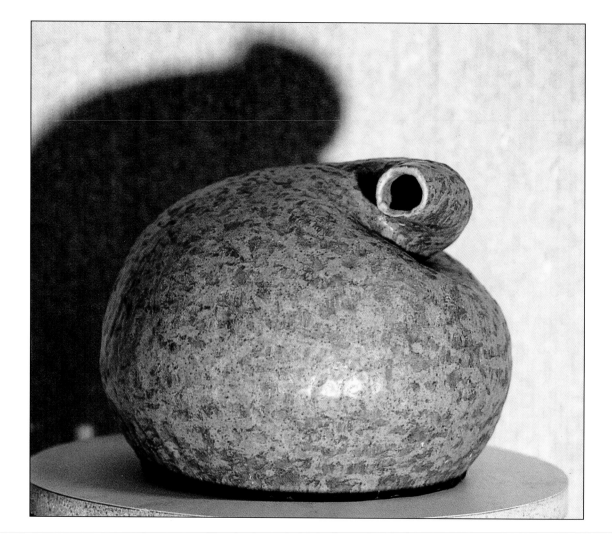

ARTIST: C. Keen Zero
TITLE: Shy Zork Pot
DIMENSIONS: 9" x 13"
MATERIALS/TECHNIQUES: Stoneware,
hand built

Daphne Roehr Hatcher

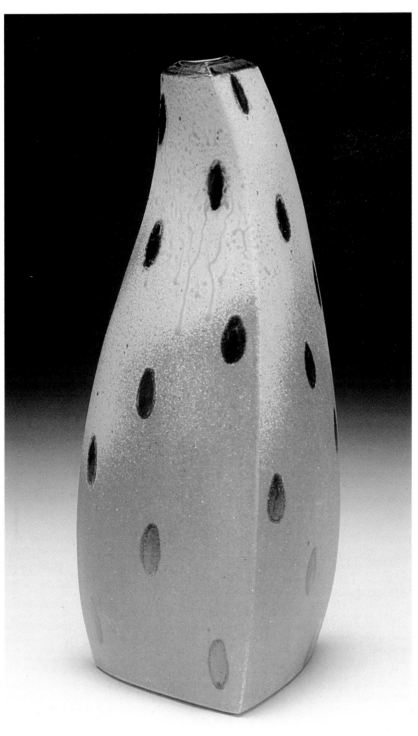

Photo: Robert Langham III

ARTIST: Daphne Roehr Hatcher
TITLE: Spotted Vase
DIMENSIONS: 19" x 9" x 9"
MATERIALS/TECHNIQUES: Stoneware,
wood fired, slab construction

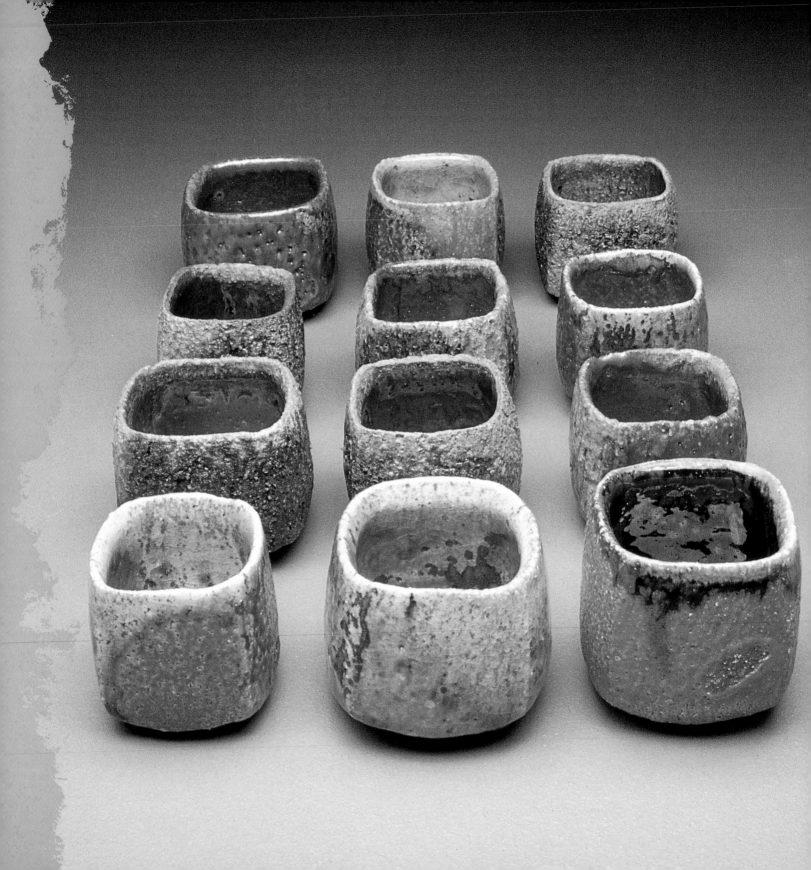

TEAPOTS, PITCHERS & DRINKING VESSELS

In the fine art of the pouring and drinking vessel, artists are interpreting classical ceramic forms in the most individualistic ways. Their teapots, pitchers and drinking vessels often take on elaborate shapes, with surface decorations that bring them to life.

No other ceramic object attracts as much attention and discussion as the teapot. The parts of a teapot which give us its character — spout, handle, lid and body — are endlessly variable. Artists emphasize the linear elements of spout and handle to make the most of spatial suggestibility. Lids can surprise us, and the body must be able to stand in its on space and command proper respect.

In the process of giving physical substance to the concept of form, artists continue to wrestle with the design challenges of function. It is the correct relationship of the parts which gives the work its vitality. The best pieces achieve a kind of magic — they seem to dance across the countertop, asking to be picked up!

Generally, cups sit on the table. But the hand knows that there can be a quiet beauty in everyday objects; these drinking vessels also seem to be humble visitors from another time. They have strong personal associations to which we can easily relate.

Whether the object is for functional use, quiet contemplation, social protest or purely sensual beauty, it is the product of an artist's devotion to and expansion of an ageless art form. We learn from them that there is always room for new ideas in these most familiar of objects.

Mark Tomczak

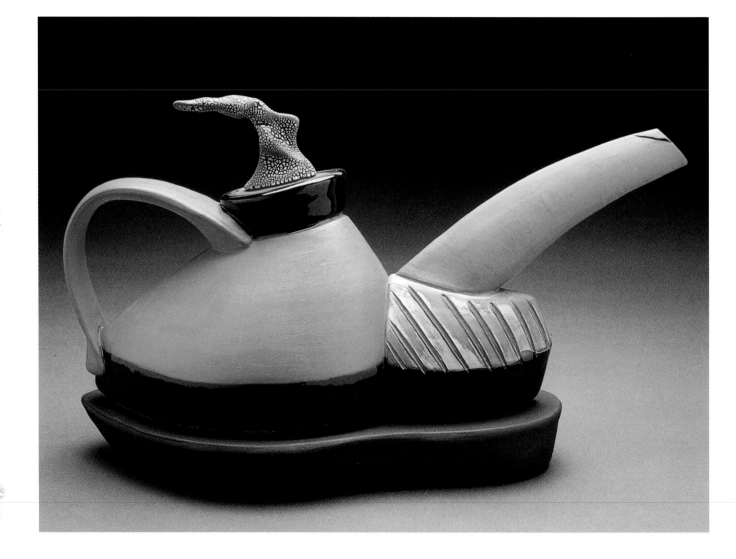

ARTIST: Mark Tomczak
TITLE: Tug Pot #1
DIMENSIONS: 5.5" x 8.5" x 4.5"
MATERIALS/TECHNIQUES: Earthenware,
thrown, altered

Lana Wilson

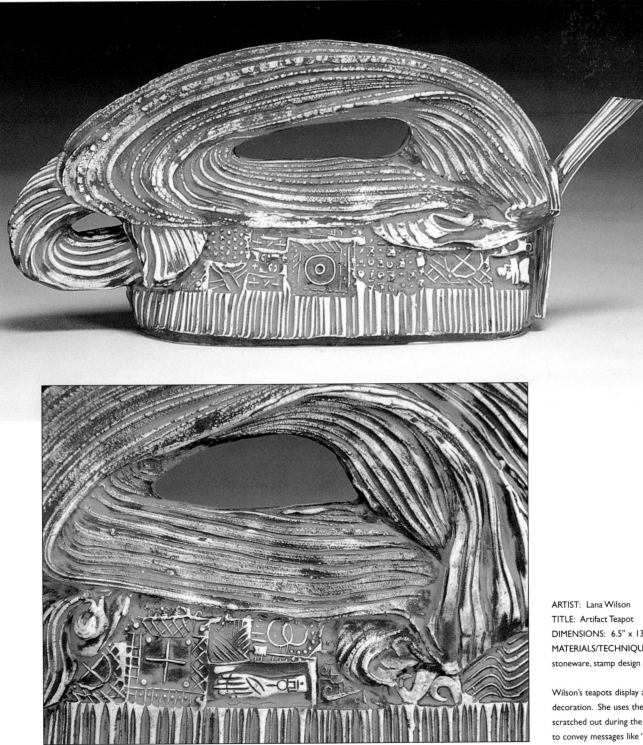

ARTIST: Lana Wilson
TITLE: Artifact Teapot
DIMENSIONS: 6.5" x 13.5" x 3"
MATERIALS/TECHNIQUES: White stoneware, stamp design

Wilson's teapots display a rich surface decoration. She uses the symbols hobos scratched out during the Great Depression to convey messages like "Don't give up."

Barbara L. Frey

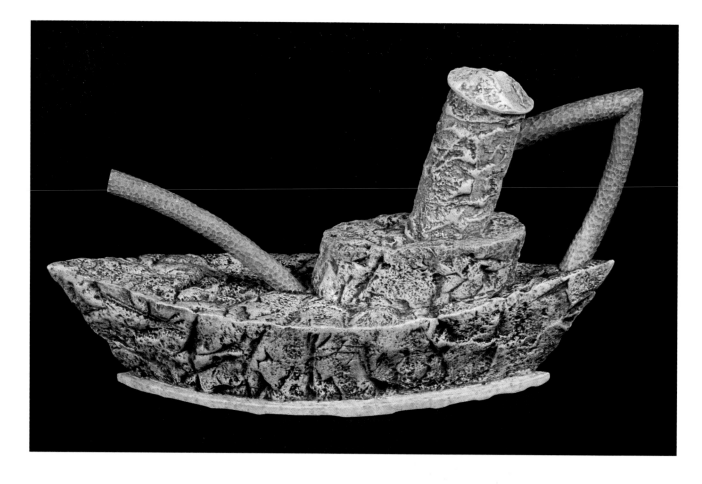

ARTIST: Barbara L. Frey
TITLE: Settle Down Teapot #15
DIMENSIONS: 5.75" x 9.5" x 3.25"
MATERIALS: Porcelain, colored porcelain,
slip, stains, glaze
TECHNIQUES: Hand built, press-molded
surface materials

Frey rewards the intimacy of experiencing
a small-scale piece by providing the viewer
with a lot to explore. The reading can
change from indentifying the form as a
"boat" to discovering landscape, shoreline,
ravine, crevasse, weathered architecture,
etc. as one explores the surface.

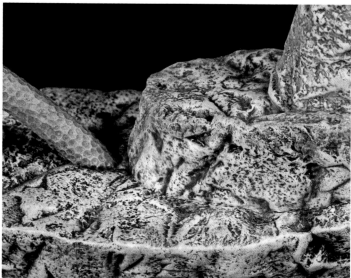

Photos: T. C. Eckersley

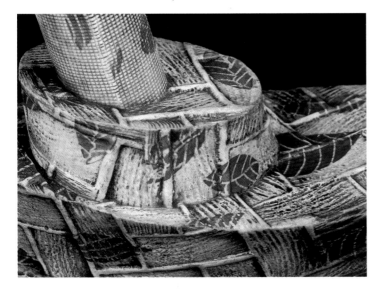

ARTIST: Barbara L. Frey
TITLE: Settle Down Teapot #18
DIMENSIONS: 5.75" x 9.25" x 3.25"
MATERIALS: Porcelain colored porcelain,
slip, stains, glaze
TECHNIQUES: Hand built, press molded
surface materials

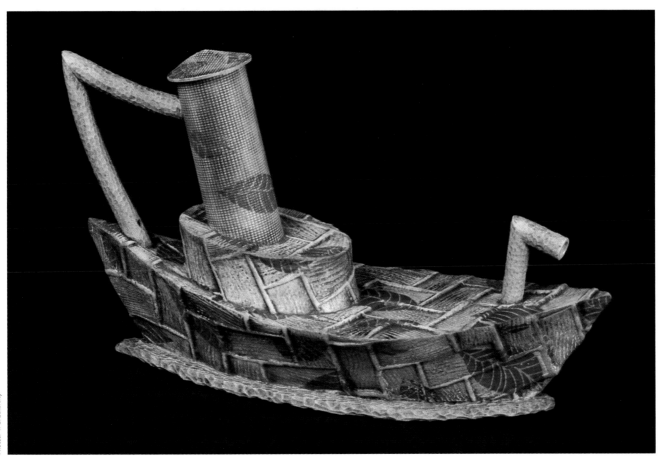

Photos: T. C. Eckersley

Susan Beiner

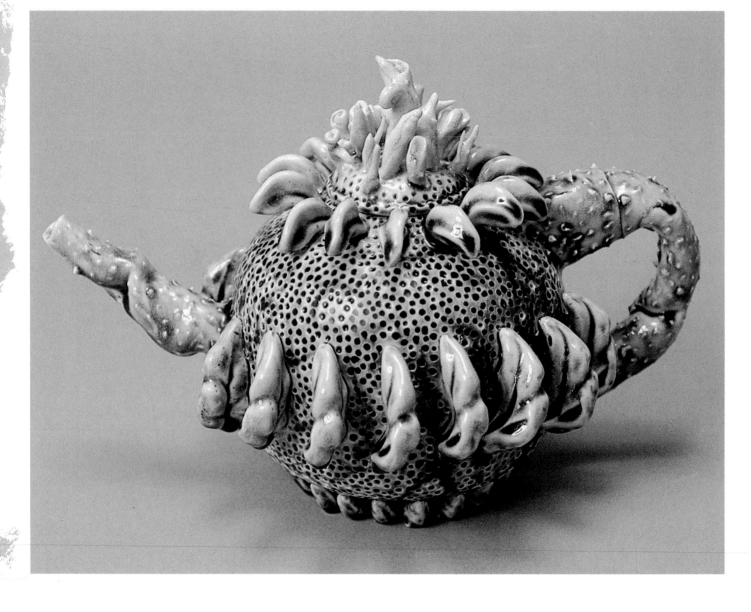

ARTIST: Susan Beiner
TITLE: Leaf Spotted Teapot
DIMENSIONS: 7" x 9" x 6"
MATERIALS/TECHNIQUES: Porcelain,
hand built, slip cast

Nancy Barbour

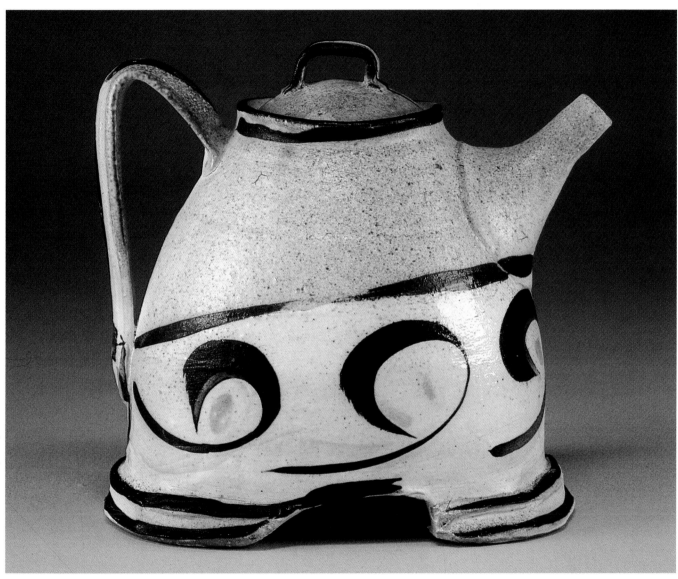

ARTIST: Nancy Barbour

TITLE: Fire

DIMENSIONS: 7" x 9" x 3"

MATERIALS/TECHNIQUES: Wood-fired stoneware

Barbour believes that the use of beautiful objects in our everyday lives can elevate the routine to a more enriching and cermonial level.

Peter Pinnell

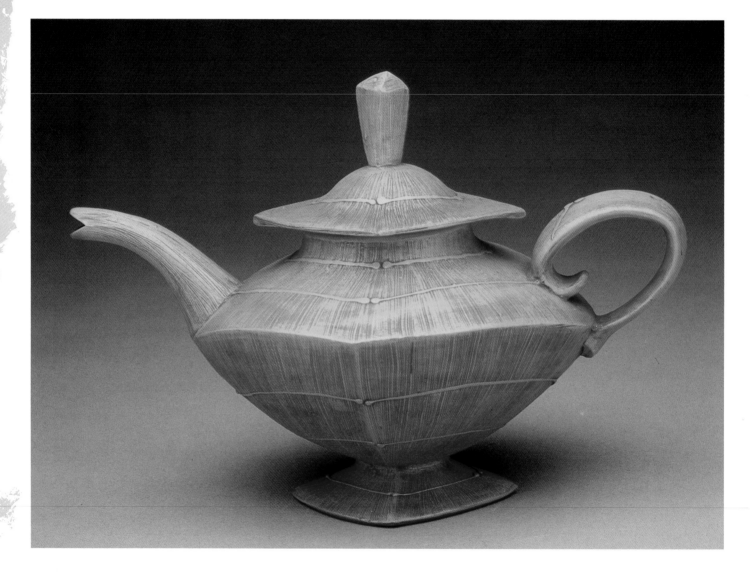

ARTIST: Peter Pinnell
TITLE: Straw Teapot
DIMENSIONS: 7" x 11" x 5"
MATERIALS/TECHNIQUES: Earthenware,
thrown, altered

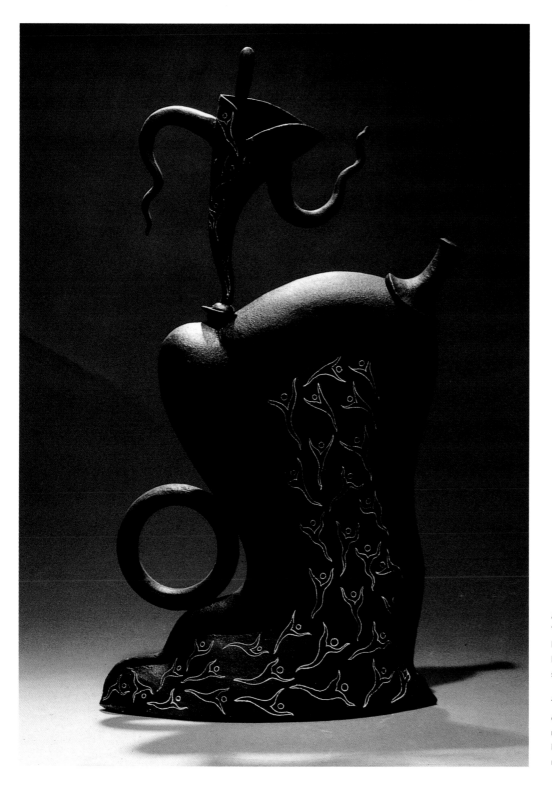

ARTIST: Michael D. Torre
TITLE: The Locomotion of Angels
DIMENSIONS: 13" x 6" x 3"
MATERIALS/TECHNIQUES: White
stoneware, black slip

Torre's work represents figures in motion
or engaged in some type of dance move-
ments. His surfaces also imply motion.
In this teapot, the torso of the figure is
removable and represents a cup.

Russell Wrankle

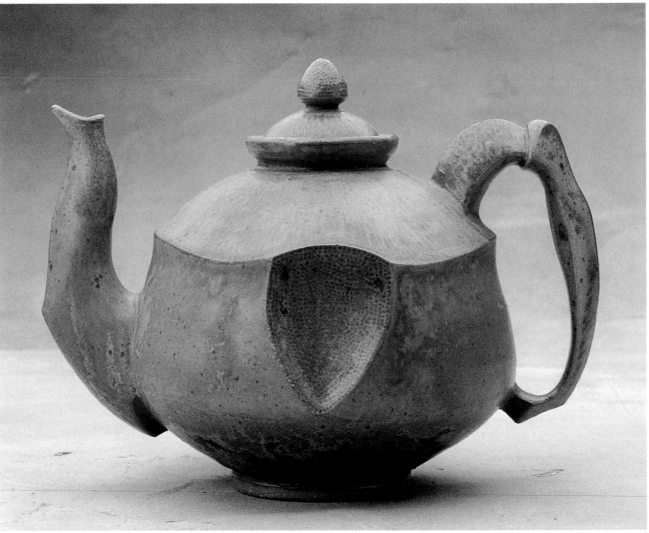

Photo: Trent Foltz

ARTIST: Russell Wrankle
TITLE: Teapot
DIMENSIONS: 6" x 8" x 6.5"
MATERIALS: Stoneware
TECHNIQUES: Wheel thrown, altered

Russell Wrankle

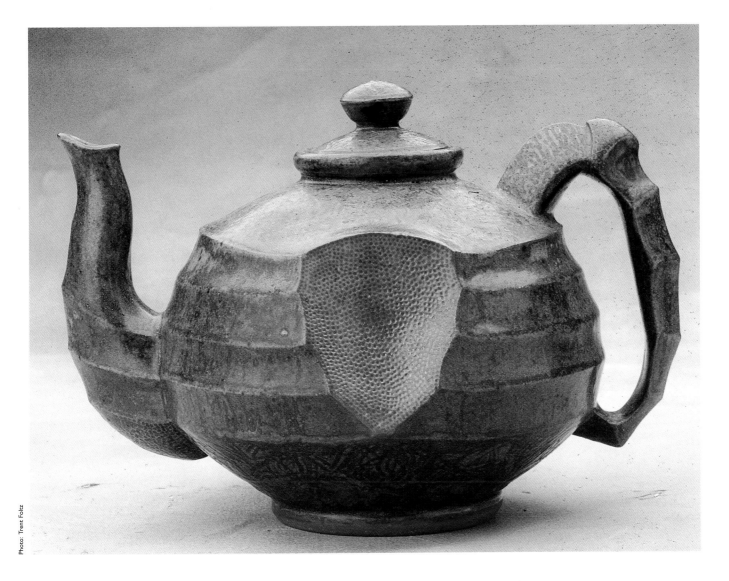

Photo: Trent Foltz

ARTIST: Russell Wrankle
TITLE: Teapot
DIMENSIONS: 6" x 8" x 6.5"
MATERIALS: Stoneware
TECHNIQUES: Wheel thrown, altered

Wendy Dubin

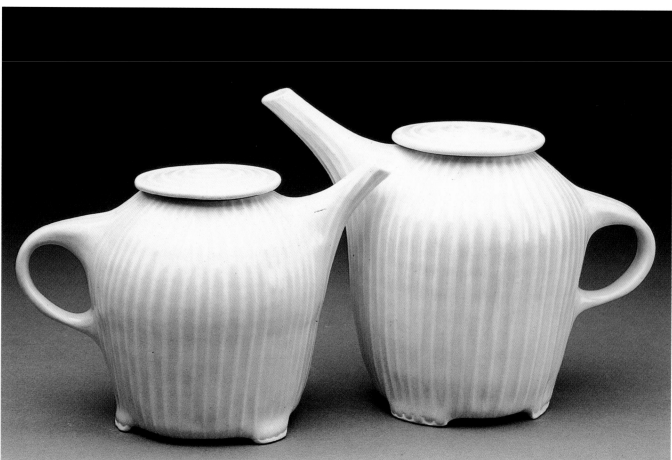

Photo: Ken Lax

ARTIST: Wendy Dubin
TITLE: Coffee & Tea Set
DIMENSIONS: teapot 5" x 7" x 4.25"
coffee 6" x 7.75" x 4.75"
MATERIALS: Porcelain
TECHNIQUES: Thrown and carved

Dubin's work integrates form and surface, and consideration for the relationship of the piece to the hand of the user. She explores how texture and line can articulate form and volume.

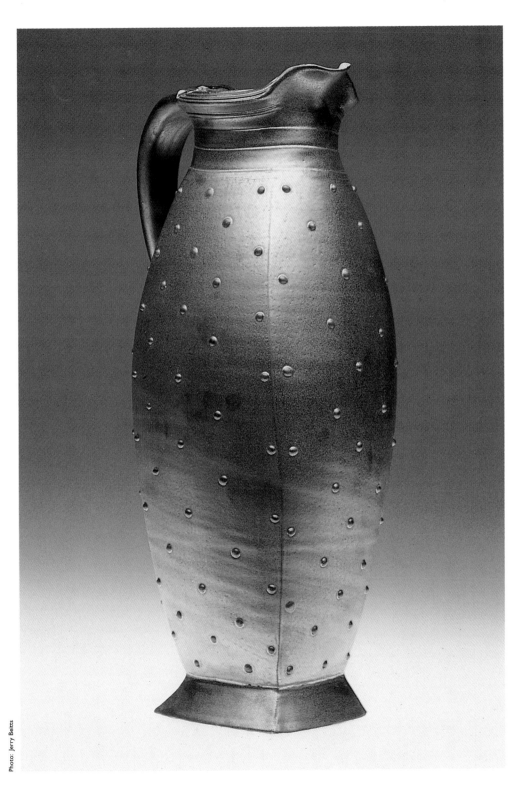

Photo: Jerry Beitts

ARTIST: Skeff Thomas
TITLE: Pitcher
DIMENSIONS: 16" x 9" x 8"
MATERIALS/TECHNIQUES: Porcelain

William A. Lucius

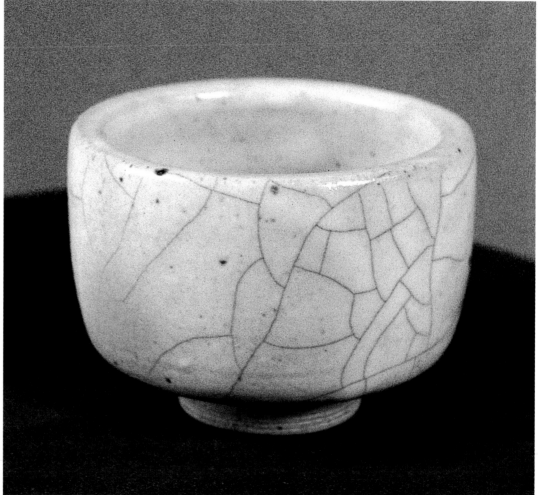

Photos: Ransom Studio

ARTIST: William A. Lucius
TITLE: Ultimate Unomi (teacup)
DIMENSIONS: 2.5" x 3" x 3"
MATERIALS: Native clay, zinc oxide glaze
TECHNIQUES: Wheel thrown, fired in
reduction atmosphere

Lucius's pottery is best understood in
terms of his professional training as a
ceramic archeologist. He uses native
rather than commercial clays, and designs
his own lead-free glazes.

Jason Hess

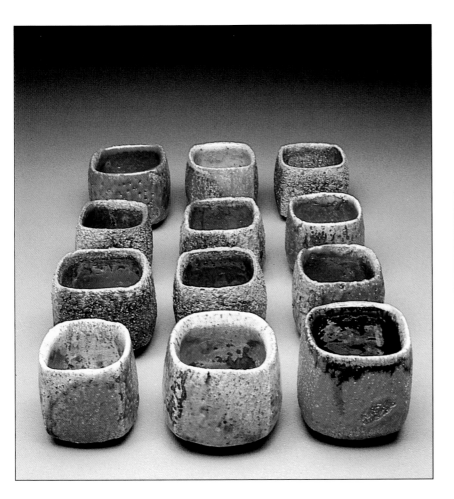

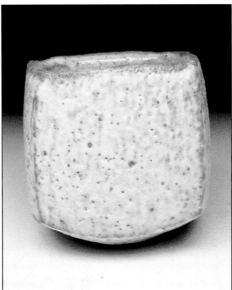

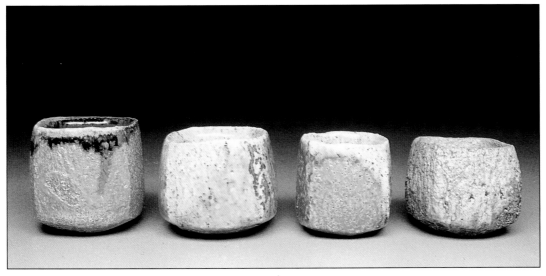

ARTIST: Jason Hess
TITLE: Twelve Whiskey Cups
DIMENSIONS: 12 cups, each 2" x 2" x 2"
MATERIALS/TECHNIQUES: Wood fired
stoneware, thrown, altered

INDEX OF ARTISTS

126

ACKNOWLEDGMENTS

This book would not be possible without the leadership of Monarch Tile, Inc. as sponsor of the Monarch National Ceramic Competition. I would especially like to thank Tom White, Monarch's President, and Barbara Broach, Director of the Kennedy-Douglass Center for the Arts, who so capably oversee this annual competition with a good dose of Southern charm. Thanks must also go to Don Traynor, who encouraged me to do this book, to Steve Bridges for his beautiful design, and to Bill Kraus for his gentle editing. Most importantly, I am grateful to the artists who generously allowed me to reproduce their photographs, and who continue to inspire me with the magic of clay. — T.S.